DOCTOR WATSON ARCHITECTS

INCOMPLETE WORKS
Volume Five

VICTORIA WATSON

An AIR Grid Publication
Copyright © 2023, Doctor VA Watson

ISBN: 9781838018030

CONTENTS

Introduction, 5

Project ONE
A New Kind of Apartment Block (1999)
6-13

Project TWO
Europan Five: Housing, Landscape, Travel & Proximity (2000)
14-29

Project THREE
Concept House 2000
30-37

Project FOUR
Landmark Tower/U2 Studio (2003)
38-43

Project FIVE
Salt Housing Block (2004)
44-55

Project SIX
Lunar Leap (2004)
56-65

Project SEVEN
A New Skyscraper Concept (2005)
66-71

...But, if it seems possible that Roussel did bury a secret message in his work, it seems equally likely that no one will ever succeed in finding out what it is. What he leaves us with is a work that is like the perfectly preserved temple of a cult which has disappeared without a trace, or a complicated set of tools whose use cannot be discovered. But even though we may never be able to 'use' his work in the way he hoped, we can still admire its inhuman beauty, and be stirred by a language that seems always on the point of revealing its secret...

John Ashbery, Introduction, Raymond Roussel, How I Wrote Certain Of My Books

Introduction

This volume of Incomplete Works gathers together a number of speculative design projects made by Doctor Watson Architects in the early years of the 21st century. Most, if not all, of the projects began as a response to a specific architectural competition brief, however, DWA never were interested in winning a competition.

An architecture competition is distinguished from a direct commission by the simultaneous attention to the same project by competing architects. The whole point of the competition process is to select a 'winner' and from the point of view of the competing architects, it is only the winner who stands a chance of going on to author a building and/or place. Although DWA were pleased if their entry attracted attention and was exhibited and/or published, nevertheless the fact that they were interested in losing, not winning left DWA with considerable freedom to interpret the brief in their own unique way. By adopting this anarchistic approach DWA could use the competition brief as a ready-made device for orientating their thought, for developing a creative inquiry and for organising its output.

Over the years DWA have been asking themselves about the status of these projects, what kind of a thing are they? The projects are represented through the conventional conceptual tools and media that all architects use when they are developing a design: physical and digital models, diagrams, sketches, scale projections and perspective views. And yet, because DWA were not fully aligned with the competition programme, so there is something a little quirky and strange about the projects.

One thing that is certainly true about these projects is, they are more concerned with the medium of architectural design than they are with the content of some particular design programme. In this respect they are rather like the 'Urbino perspectives,' the set of three painted panels dating from the 15th century (one housed in the National Gallery of the Marches in Urbino, a second in the Walters Art Gallery in Baltimore and a third in the Berlin Staatliche Museum), which are generally understood as depictions of scenes of imaginary ideal cities.

The Urbino Perspectives
Top, Urbino Panel, Urbino National Gallery of the Marches
Middle, Baltimore Panel, Walters Art Gallery
Bottom, Berlin Panel, Staatliche Museum, Berlin
For more about the history of the panels and a fascinating structural analysis see Hubert Damish, The Origin of Perspective, The MIT Press, 1994

Project ONE: A New Kind of Apartment Block

This project began as an entry for an open competition set by the Manchester-based property developers Urban Splash. Our proposal responded to the stated objective that was to *'create a new housing type, capable of mass production, using modern building techniques at a realistic budget to challenge preconceptions laid down by volume house builders.'* But more than that, our proposal was intended as a critique of the post modern style of development that was rampant in those days.

Our proposed new housing type is organised as a single unit on one level, it is 'L' shaped in plan, and arranged around a void. Although the unit is flanked above and below and upon either side by similar, if not identical units, it has four, rather than two, external walls. But the external walls are not really walls: because the unit is structured and supported within a precast concrete frame and that means the external walls are reduced to partitions, they are light, they can slide and they are made of glass, in other words they reflect, refract and transmit light.

The precast concrete frame is articulated and exposed wherever possible (the concrete is pigmented black). There are six floors of aggregated units stacked within the entire framing armature. All units face the same way, with the 'front' opening out to the north/north-west onto a view of the surrounding environment while the 'back' facing south/south-east is closed and intersects with the vertical towers (stairs and lifts) and long, horizontal decks that constitute the building's circulation system. A short glass bridge connects each unit to the circulation system, between unit and circulation a narrow void plunges, vertiginously down to the ground.

The aggregate of units is suspended above a beautifully manicured lawn, subdivided by planting beds. The aggregate is supported on a transition floor consisting of deep beams, resting on widely spaced cylindrical columns that are set down carefully amongst the lawn and planters. The circulation system, mentioned above, is designed to be foliage-friendly, it will be made of timber trellis and meshwork with minimal steelwork for support and stability, it is coded green on the drawings.

The aggregate of units is terminated at the top and crowned by a huge topiary sculpture, clipped and trained to follow the figure of the aggregate of units below. This thick, bushy mass will have pockets of inhabitable space carved-out inside, so people can walk through it, as if they were in a baroque garden.

The units themselves consist of two basic constructional elements. First are the fixed walls and partitions, rising 2.7 meters between the floor slabs without openings; these will be of simple block construction, insulated as necessary, with plasterboard and skim. Secondly, there are the sliding glass panels which give the units their visual permeability and their spatial flexibility; these will be double glazed units sliding upon a metal track, fixed to the face of the building or concealed within the depth of the floor construction. Heating and lighting systems will be integrated into the floor construction, so all fittings can be recessed rather than revealed.

The 'L' shaped configuration means each unit has its own atrium space inside. Each atrium is bounded on two sides by full-height glass screens, on one side by a solid 'party' wall and on the fourth side by a low-level, glass balustrade (the north/north-west orientation protects the atria from direct sunlight). The ground of the atrium too is made of glass - panels supported on a grid of beams. Although the configuration of the units is flipped from one level to the next, the aggregate is designed so that the atria align vertically, one on top of the other. This stack arrangement will produce interesting light effects, reflecting, refracting and transmitting in all kinds of rich and unpredictable ways and diffusing into the interior spaces of the units. The atria will be highly sensitive to changing weather conditions, but also to the activities of the occupants, whose atrium presence will be felt by their neighbours above and below. It is inevitable that this new kind of proximity will challenge old habits of dwelling and may take a while to get used to, but in the longer term it will welcome in new forms of neighbourliness that will be beneficial and valuable.

Each unit displays a decorative monochrome panel on its front, outward looking face; taken together, these panels bring vibrancy to the appearance of the block within the urban context.

Figure 1/1. View approaching along the canal side from the south

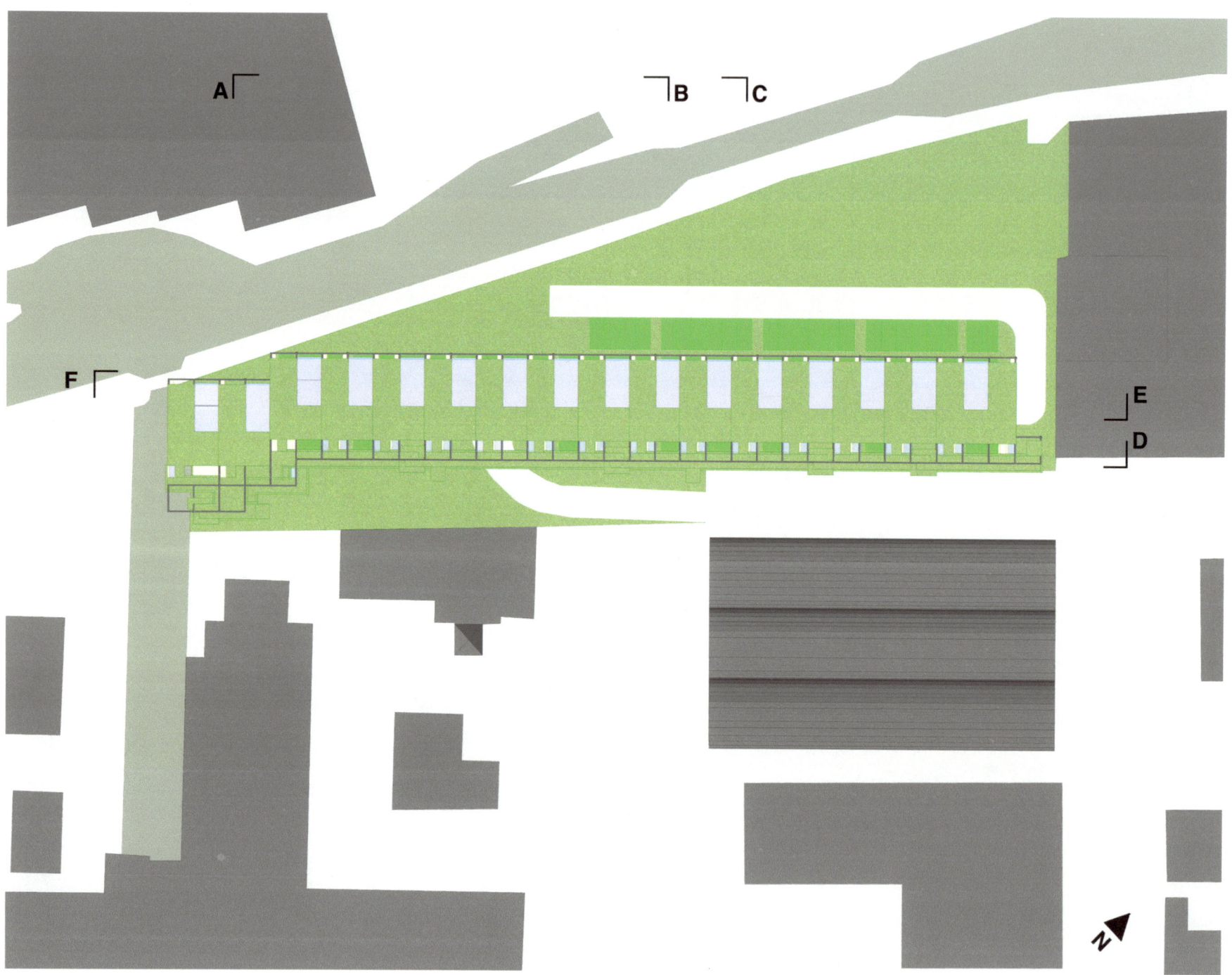

Figure 1/2. Roof Plan with north point and section indicators

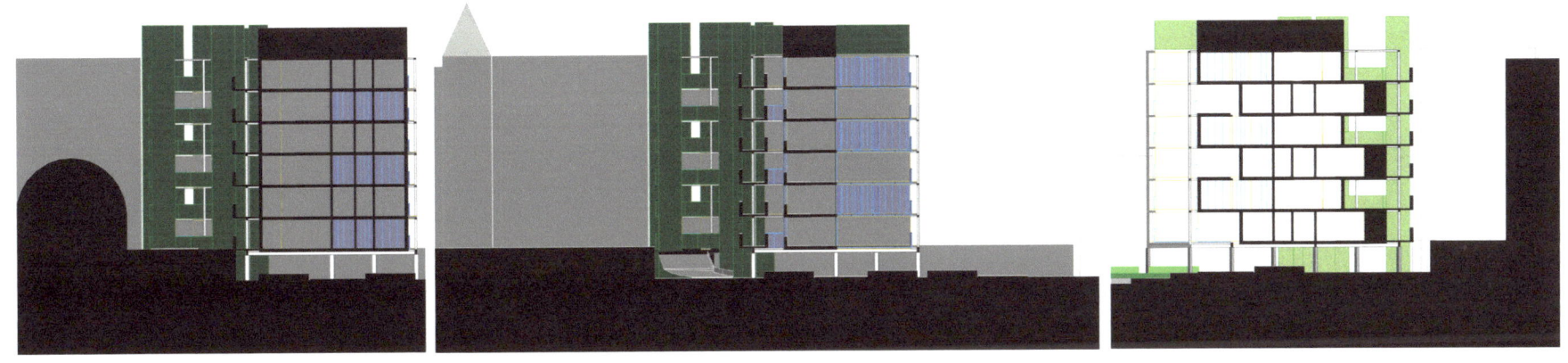
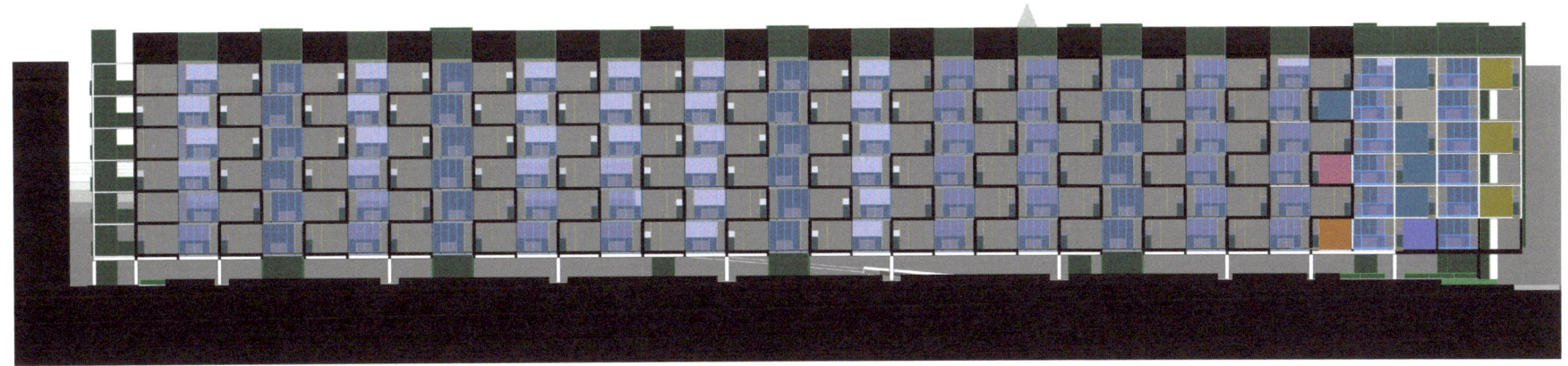

Figure 1/3. Sections CC, BB, AA above; section FF below

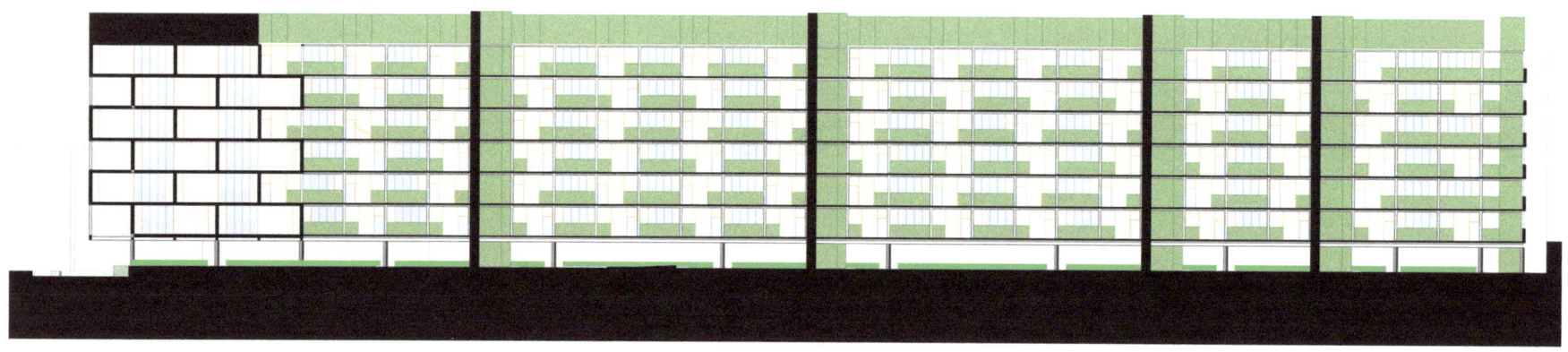

Figure 1/4. Section DD above; section EE below

Figure 1/5. Plan diagrams, top left, undercroft; top right, L1; bottom left, L2,4&6; bottom right, L3&5

Figure 1/6. Six views from undercroft and first floor levels

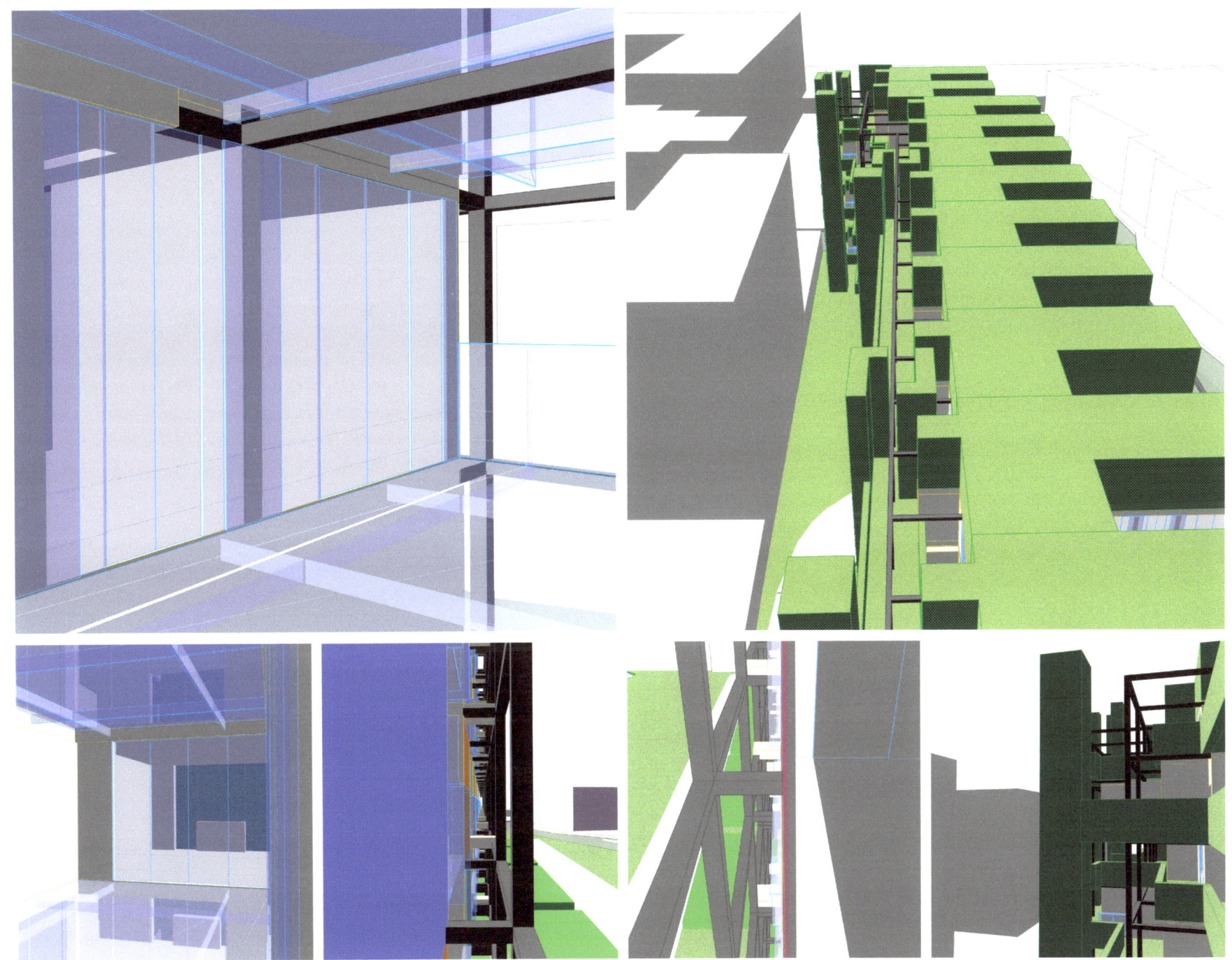

Figure 1/7. Six views, upper levels

Project TWO: Europan Five: Housing, Landscape, Travel & Proximity

This project began as an entry for Europan Five: new housing, landscape, travel and proximity (2000). The competition asked about the possibility of integrating urban complexity through architectural design, it was especially concerned with the residual spaces in towns and cities that have formed at the crossing of transport networks. We proposed a scheme for the given site on the Manor House Estate in Sheffield.

Prompted by the competition brief, the proposal considered the following factors: 1) Topography; 2) Infrastructure; 3) Opportunity; 4) Environmental Design

TOPOGRAPHY
What was striking about the Manor House Estate was the disjuncture between 'building' and 'nature,' as if each were embarrassed by the presence of the other. The pronounced fall of the land gave rise to dramatic panoramic views out and beyond the immediate proximity of the site and yet the layout of the houses seemed to ignore this natural advantage, demonstrating instead a kind of shy, introverted intimacy - semi-detached houses clustered around a 'cul-de-sac.' Each house was limited and defined within its own legal property boundary by a garden fence, or hedge (figure 2/1).

Although our proposed Pandinus house types would not have been visible as an object qua house, they were nevertheless designed with the intention of generating a conscious occupancy of the land. In the particular circumstances of the Manor House Estate we thought the effect of living in the ground could be heightened by the ready-made circumstances in which the ground is found to be rising, or falling away (figure 2/2).

To exploit the change in level across the site we proposed to build rows of Pandinus Houses set out along the lines of the natural contours. The 30 metre change in level across the site gave rise to a natural high point where the existing community centre was located. This would become the site of our proposed new communal facility called the Cadmium Yellow Structure (figure 2/3).

INFRASTRUCTURE
The large number of cul-de-sac arrangements on the Manor House Estate had the effect of reducing the permeability of the road network to vehicular traffic and of encouraging other types of circulation, pedestrian and cyclist. However, there is a problem with this kind of arrangement as it tends to lead to a kind of 'ghettoisation.' We wanted to open up the site, to make it more permeable and to encourage mobility. Not only pedestrians and cyclists but other, as yet unimaginable forms of mobility. We wanted the rows of Pandinus Houses to have cars and/or other vehicles parked on the roof (we imagined and hoped the vehicles of the not-so-distant future would run at modest speeds and on alternative forms of energy to fossil fuels). To achieve this we had to re-imagine the relation of the roadway and roof, we took advantage of the given slope of the ground, proposing the Pandinus House is a single-aspect, single storey structure whose roof is a level terrace (roof/garden) coinciding with the datum of the public roadway (figures 2/4, 2/5, 2/6 & 2/7).

OPPORTUNITY
The Cadmium Yellow Structure is a prototype for a new kind of environment that will serve as a site of opportunity for places where people, communities and their visitors live. The precise form of any CY structure would depend upon the real circumstances of the place where it is built. Our provisional representation of the CY in these drawings demonstrates the principles of elemental design and assembly that would be adopted for the formulation of any CY structure (figure 2/8).

ENVIRONMENTAL DESIGN

<u>Passive Environmental Control</u>

1. Energy retrieval & sun-shading (figure 2/9):
1/a The entrance porch to the Pandinus House is on the roof, it presents a large surface of glass orientated towards the direction of the sun (south). On cold sunny days the volume of air inside the porch will warm up, this air

can be pumped down into the interior of the house by the action of a fan.

1/b A Pandinus House is orientated either east or west and opens on one side into the garden. This boundary is mediated by a narrow zone of space enclosed within a double system of sliding glass partitions. On cold sunny days air within the zone will warm up, the zone will act as a kind of blanket, keeping the inside of the house warm.

1/c For protection from solar gain on hot sunny days, all elements of the enclosing system made from glass will carry a sun-shading device.

2. Daylight (figure 2/10):

2/a The roof of the Pandinus House has several openings encased, or enclosed, in a construction of glass (roof-lights). These allow daylight to permeate through into the secluded rooms at the back of the house.

2/b Both the porch and garden zone already mentioned in section 1 above will allow daylight to permeate through into the interior of the house.

2/c Some of the interior partitions will be made of a translucent material that encourages the diffusion of natural light inside the house.

3. Ventilation: (figure 2/11):

3/a The roof-lights mentioned in 2/a above will have a built-in tilting louvre mechanism and they will have opening lights. The garden zone mentioned in 1/b and 2/b above will consist of a system of glass panels that can assume a variety of relationships within the limiting conditions of 'all panels open' and 'all panels closed.' Between these extremes there is a rich variety of possibilities, allowing the house to adjust and accommodate changing needs and desires for the circulation of air.

4. Heat-loss (figure 2/13):

4/a Solid walls are well insulated and uninterrupted by openings so heat-loss from these will be negligible.

4/b Concerning the garden zone referred to in 1/b above. During daylight hours it is likely the occupants of the house will want partial or even full transparency to the outside. Although the glass units that make up the screen will be double glazed, at certain times of the year there will be considerable heat loss through this element of the building fabric. The introduction of an under floor system of electrical or hot-water heating into the garden zone will go some way to alleviate the problem of heat-loss from this part of the building. At night time, curtains or blinds can be pulled across the glazed screens.

4/c Surface 6, the roof garden, is a well insulated element but is has roof-lights set into it, as mentioned in 2/1 above, these will be double-glazed units. The inhabitants of the house are likely to desire the full benefits of daylight coming from the roof-lights and will be reluctant to cover them over in the daylight hours, however, at night they can be covered-over by ceiling hatches or blinds.

Water Re-cycling

The Pandinus house is designed to use water more than just once (figure 2/14). First, rainwater is stored in a large-diameter (approx 25m3 capacity) tank. This is used to flush the toilet. Second, grey water is pumped to a small-diameter (approx 11m3 capacity) tank with coil to preheat mains water for H/W cylinder. Overflow grey water is taken to the sewage system, but may also be drawn-off for watering the garden (it could also supply a low-temperature under-floor heating option). Third, as an optional refinement, the occupier can install a heat-pump in place of the coil heat-exchanger in the grey water tank, reducing demand for supplementary energy.

Landscape

1. Earthworks

One very important feature of a Pandinus house is that it is built into the landscape and that several of them in combination will form a terrace. To build a terrace requires moving a considerable amount of earth around. In principle we envisage the earthwork will be organised across a horizontal datum (marked as Z axis on figure 2/4) and that the amount of earth taken from below Z will be equivalent to the amount of earth piled above it.

2. Roof garden

The roof garden of the Pandinus house is also the 'public face' of the building; it serves not only as a place to park but also as a front garden. It is envisaged, the occupant of each house will have strong ideas about how they want to enjoy their roof garden, however, as a basic provision each roof will be finished with a layer of topsoil over laid upon a fine metallic grid; the topsoil will encourage local flora to grow and, particularly for those who are not so keen on gardening, the mesh will provide a semblance of order.

3. Garden
Sunken and secluded at the back of the house, who is to say how the occupants will use their back gardens?

4. Roadway
The terraces of Pandinus houses face one another across a roadway, it serves as the means of access for pedestrians, cyclists and motorised vehicles. For visual delight and in order to discourage dangerous driving, most of the road surface will have a cobbled finish, but there will be bands of a smoother textured material inset amongst the cobbles, marking out a passageway for cyclists, pedestrians, prams, etc,.

Public Image

Although the primary purpose of the Cadmium Yellow Structure is to provide a place for events, the building design does take environmental factors into consideration and includes small windmills, waste-collection banks and colourful signage (as indicated on figure 2/8). The windmills are miniature versions of the types used in wind farming. They will be functional, but their primary role is symbolic. The waste collection banks are an integral part of a localised system of credit intended to reward and thereby to encourage waste retrieval. Creditors will pay less for using the facilities of the CY structure, for example the cost of renting the dance hall might be off-set against the return of empty bottles. Signs and signage is an important aspect of the Cadmium Yellow image, it should be loud and colourful. The bumptious look of the CY structure will announce the facilities available within it and act as lively visual stimulant within the local environment (figures 2/16 & 2/17).

Figure 2/1. Plan of the site area. 1. layout of proposed new Pandinus Houses; 2. Cadmium Yellow Structure; 3. proposed new cycle and pedestrian pathway. 4. existing semi-detached houses clustered around 'cul-de-sac' type road and pathways

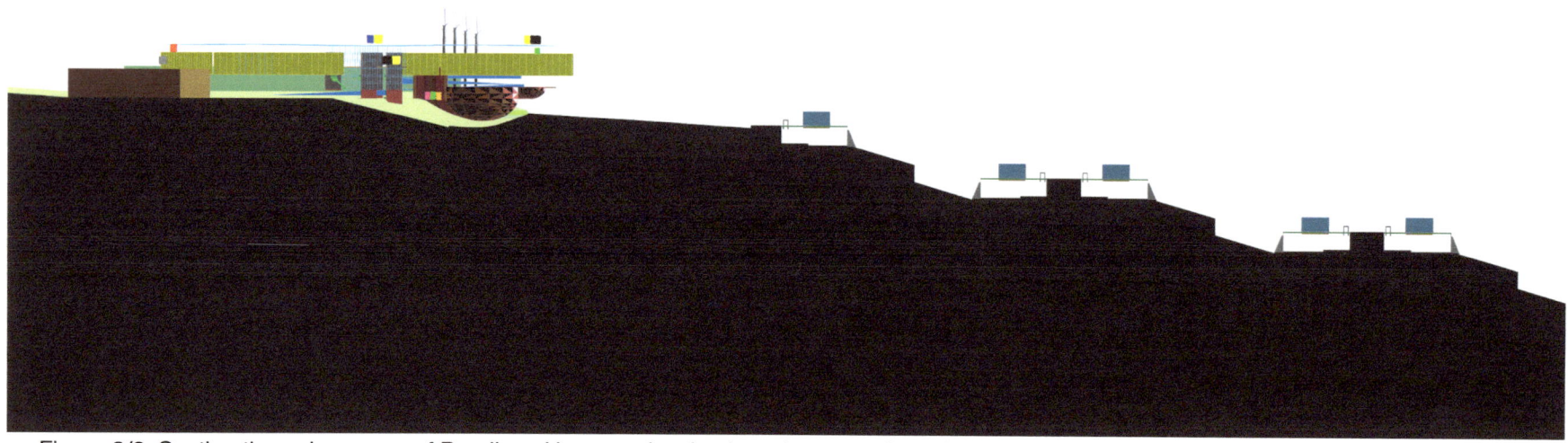

Figure 2/2. Section through a range of Pandinus Houses, showing how they are adapted to the natural contours of the site, with Cadmium Yellow Structure perched on the ridge at the top

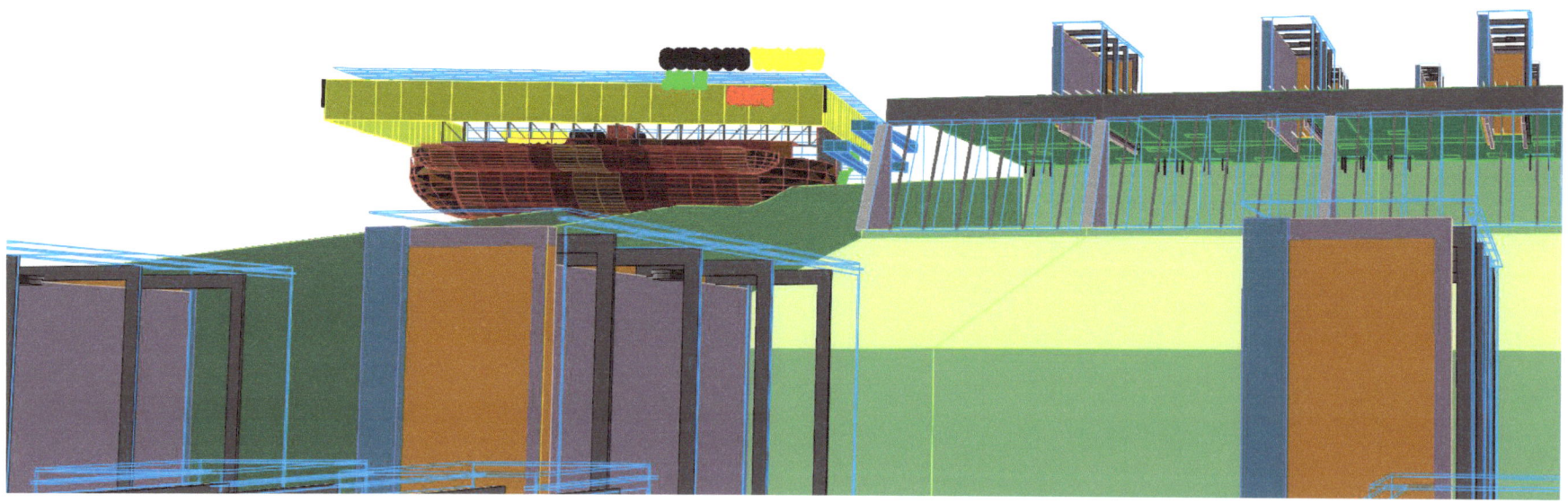

Figure 2/3. View across the terraces of Pandinus Houses toward the Cadmium Yellow Structure

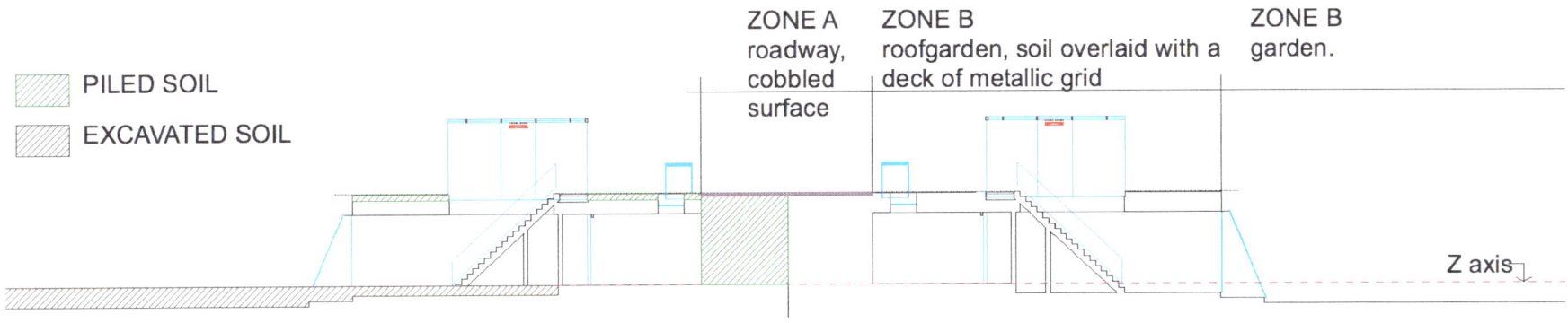

Figure 2/4. Section-diagram through a pair of Pandinus Houses separated by the public roadway at roofgarden/entry level. The section indicates how 'piled' and 'excavated' soil will be redistributed about a common axis Z

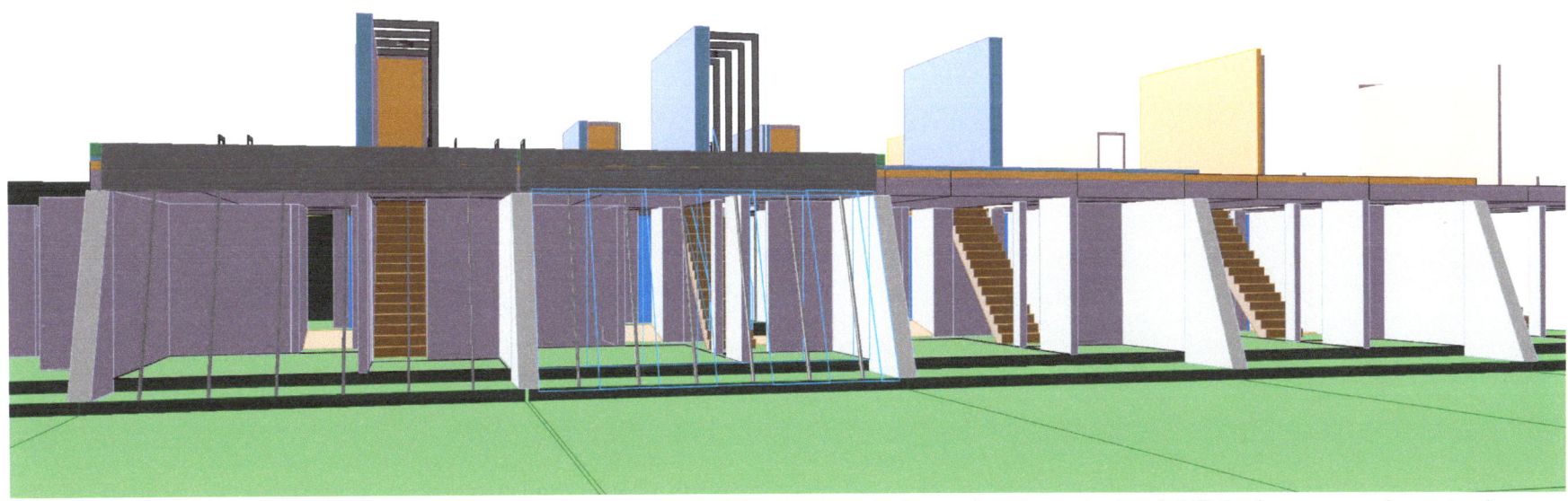

Figure 2/5. An array of Pandinus Houses, looking from the level of the Z axis up to the roofgarden/entry level (NB the houses are drawn to show different phases of construction, only the second from the left is complete)

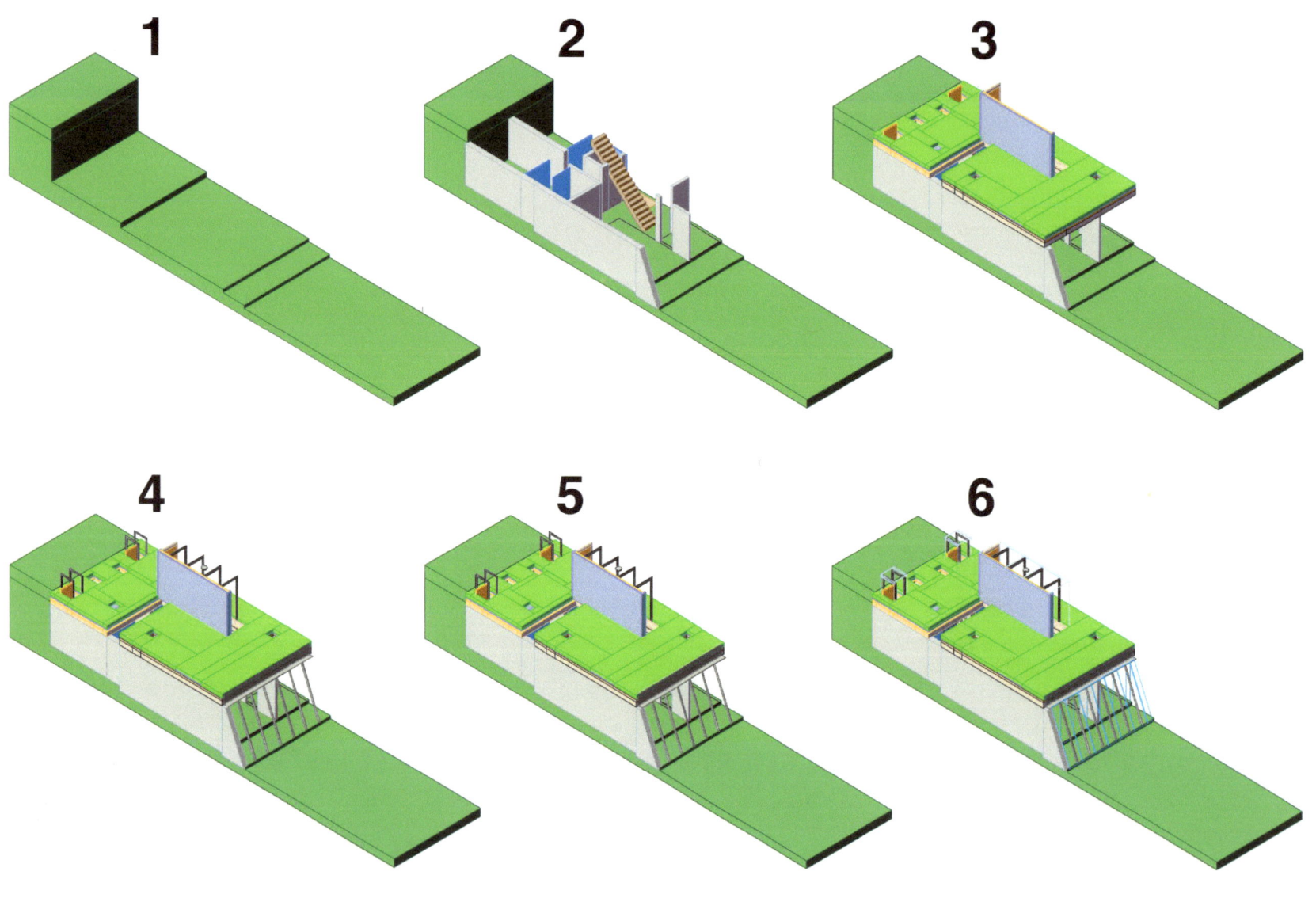

Figure 2/6. The elements and assembly sequence of a Pandinus House. 1. base; 2. walls & stairway; 3. roof garden; 4&5. framing; 6. glass panels

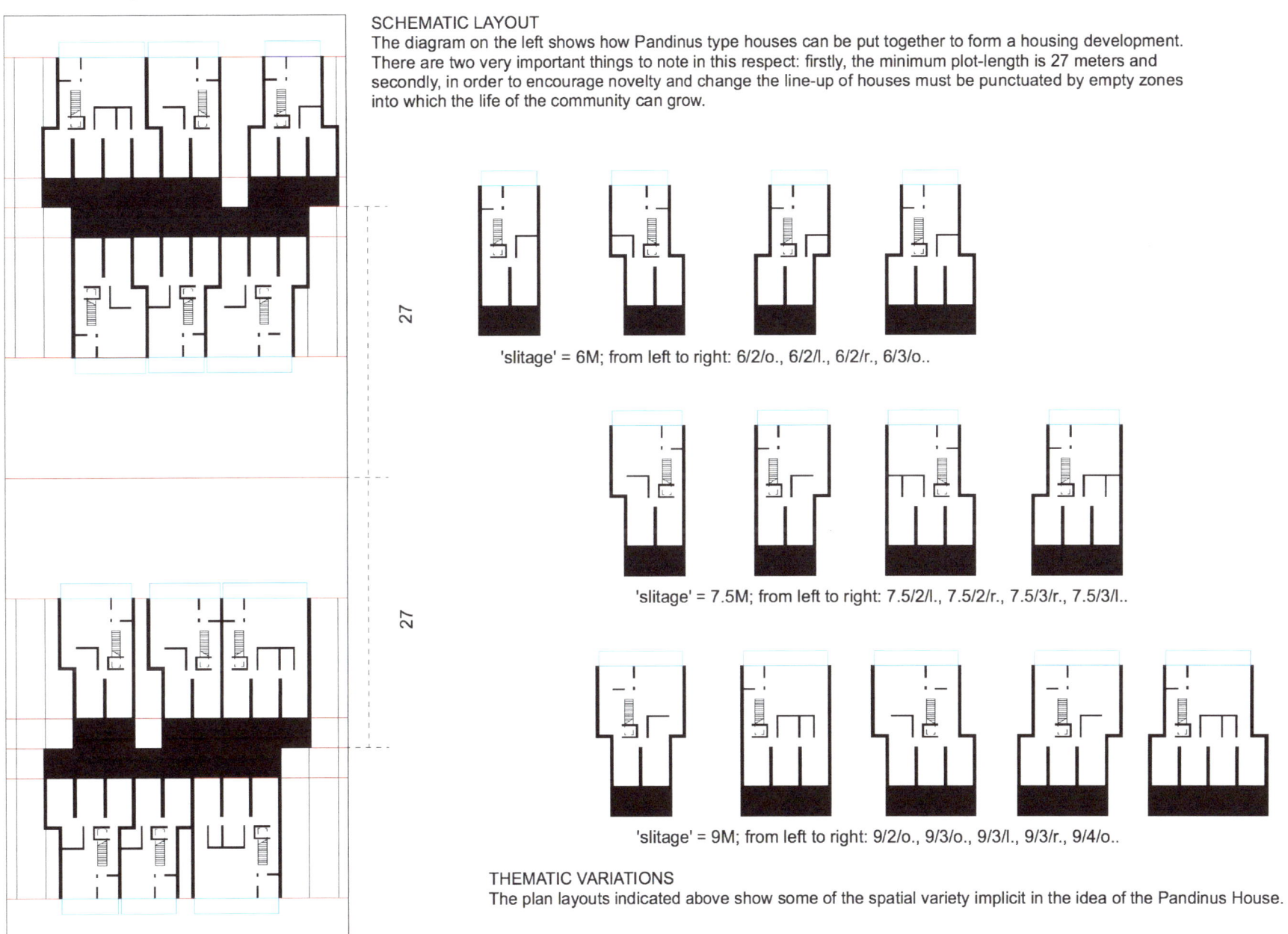

Figure 2/7. Pandinus House plan types and combinations

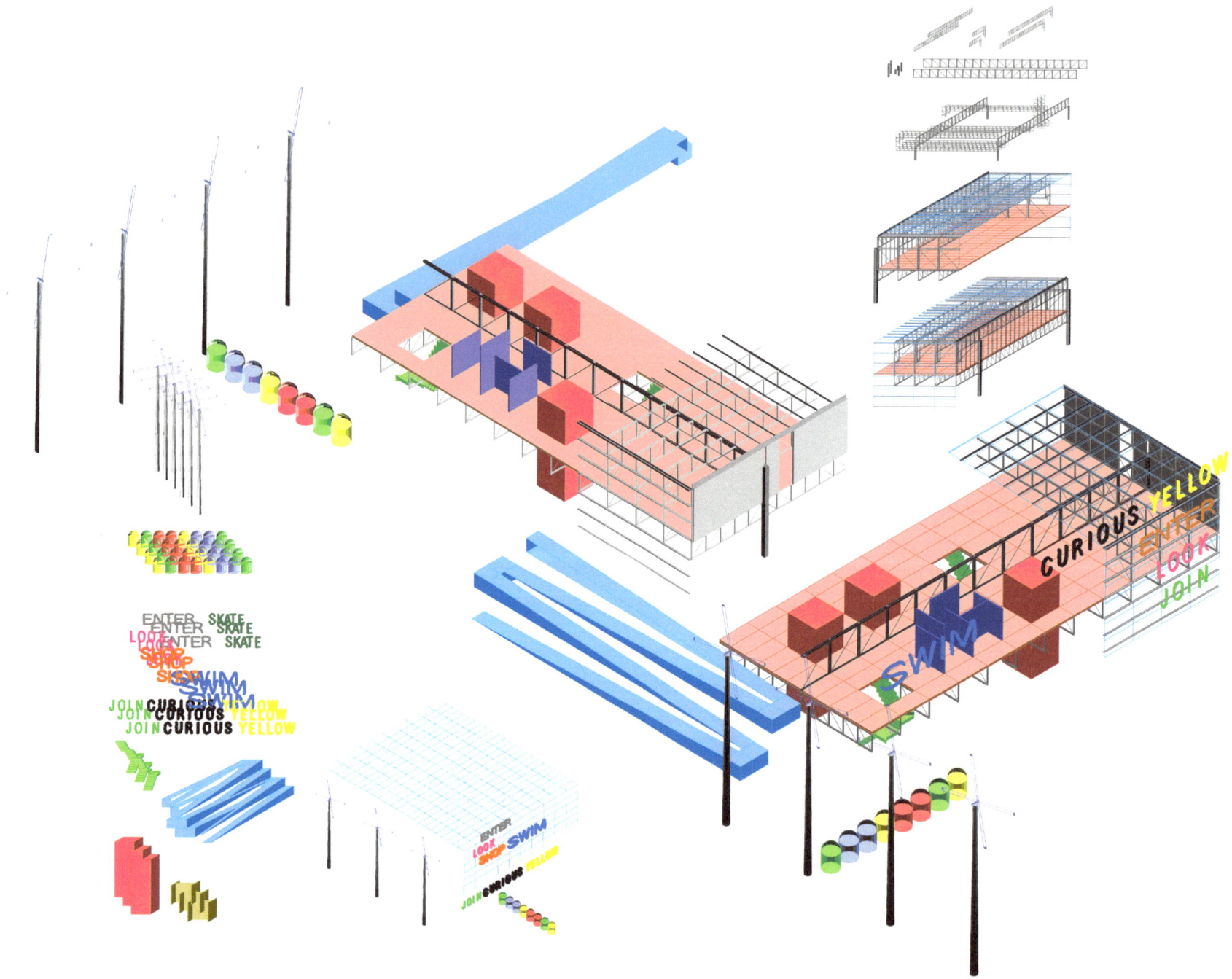

Figure 2/8. Elemental components of the Cadmium Yellow Structure

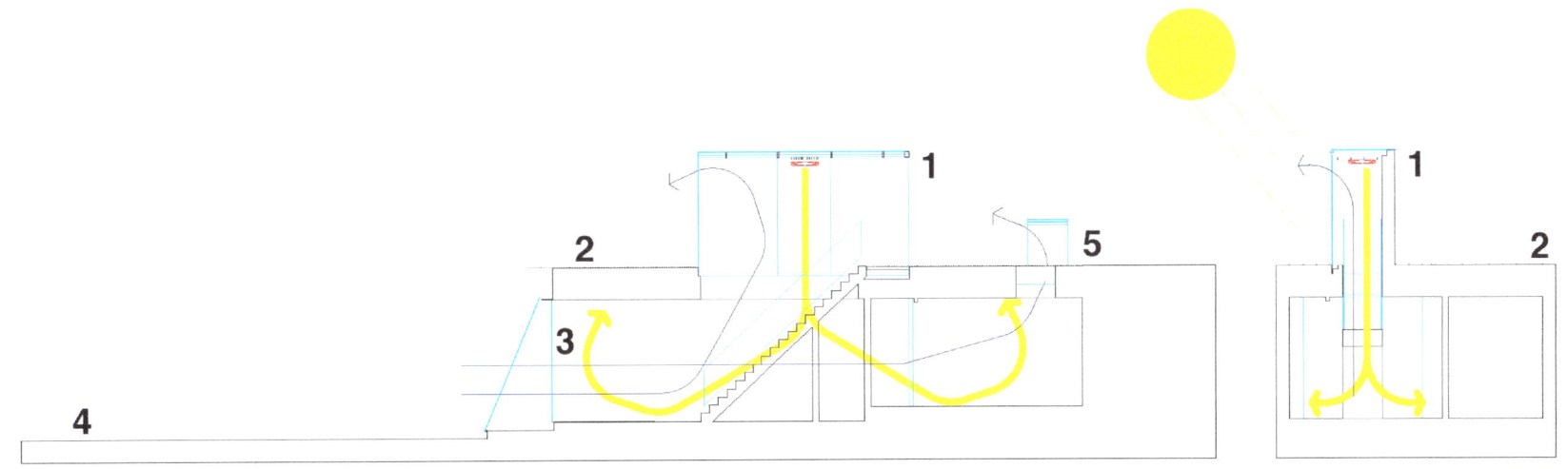

Figure 2/9. Section-diagram through the short and long dimension of the Pandinus House, 1. porch; 2. roof; 3. mediating zone; 4. garden; 5. roof light

Figure 2/10. View across the roof-tops of Pandinus Houses showing an array of entrance porches and roof-lights (NB the houses are drawn to show different phases of construction)

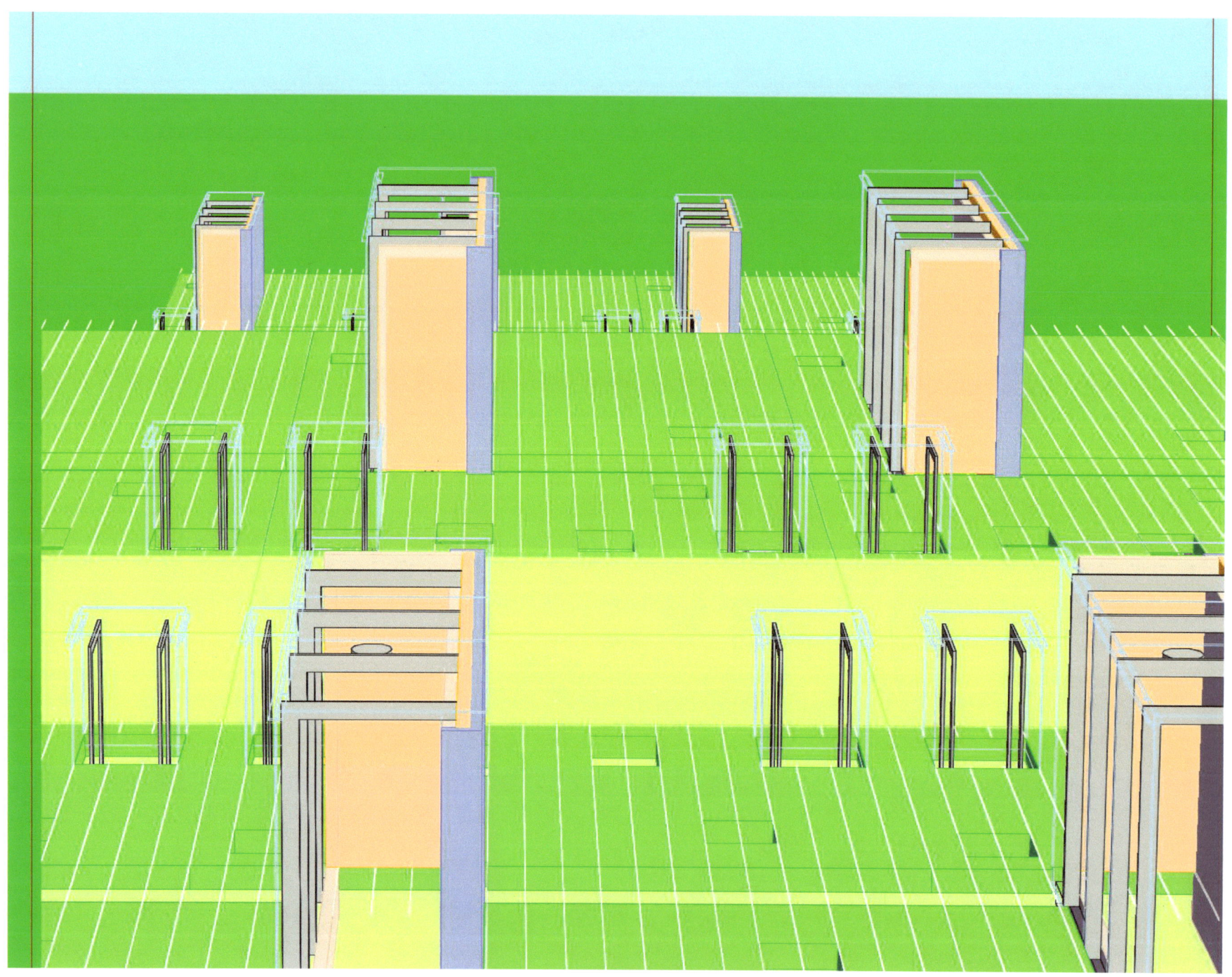

Figure 2/11. Perspective view showing patterning of entry porches and roof-lights laid out on the roof-top of an array of Pandinus Houses

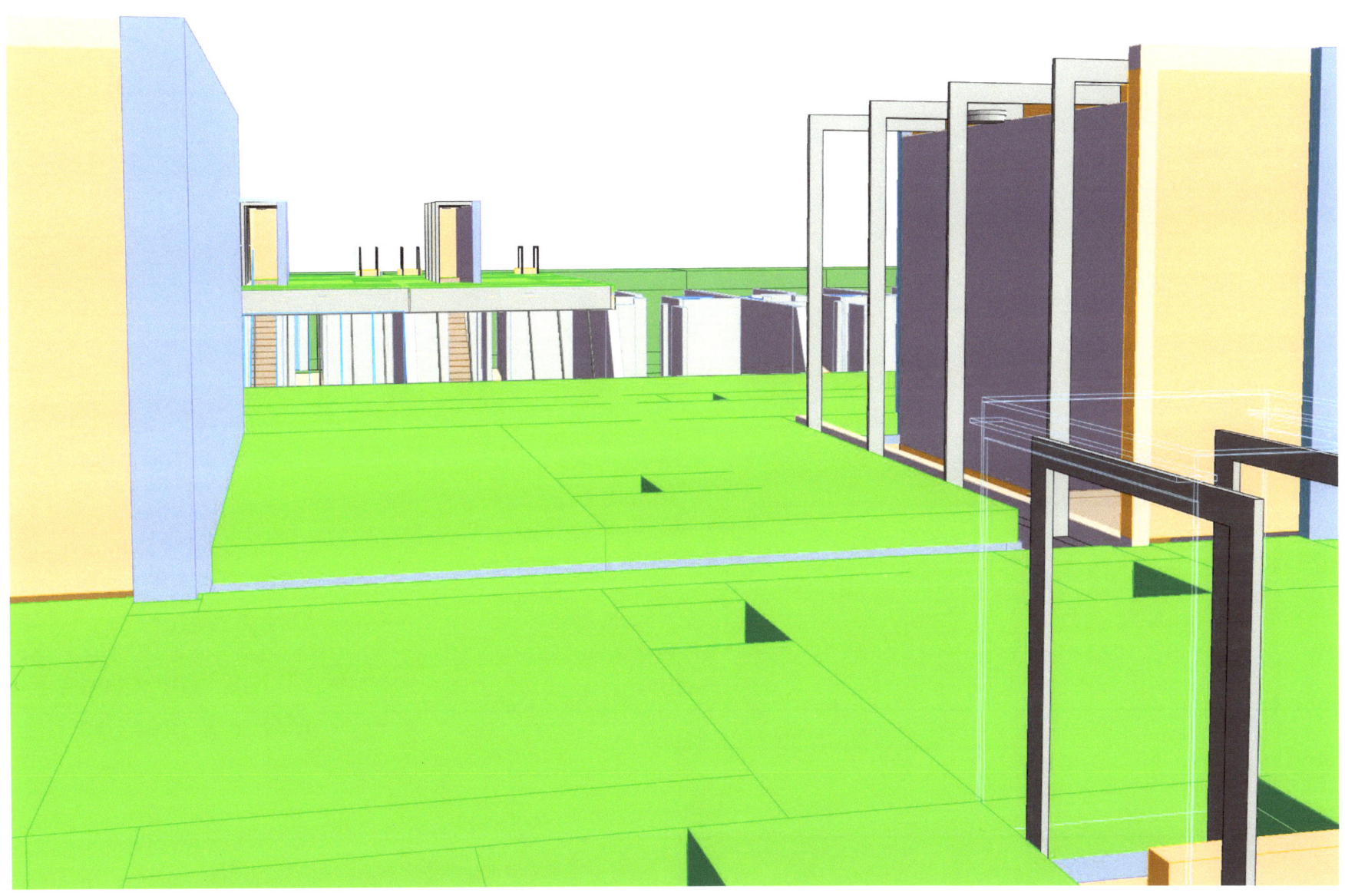

Figure 2/12. Perspective view looking across the roof-tops towards garden parapet (NB the houses are drawn to show different phases of construction)

	COST		ENERGY			OPENINGS		WATER	NOTES
	MATERIALS	CONSTRUCTION	EMBODIED	THERMAL CONDUCTANCE	ACTIVATE RENEWABLE SOURCE	DAYLIGHT	VENTILATION	UTILISE RE-CYCLING	
SURFACE 1 Rear retaining wall	-1	+1	-1	-1	0	0	0	+	re-use excavated soil from garden side. Light-weight concrete fill (as necessary) sheet metal retaining structure, waterproof layer, insulation, blockwall, internal finish
SURFACE 2 Ground floor	-1	+1	-1	-1	0	0	0	0	suspended floor - PC floor beams & infill blocks, insulation, screed, internal finish
SURFACE 3 Boundary wall	-1	-1	-1	-1	0	0	0	0	Insulated brick or block cavity wall
SURFACE 4 Boundary wall	-1	-1	-1	-1	0	0	0	0	Insulated brick or block cavity wall
SURFACE 5 Garden screen	+1	1	+1	+1	+	+	+	0	Double glazed units on lightweight steel frame
SURFACE 6 Roof garden	+1	+1	1	-1	+	+	+	+	Metal grid, 200mm topsoil, ballast, profiled meta decking, 150mm insulation, (to falls) Pc floor beams & infill blocks, internal finish

Figure 2/13. Building fabric study

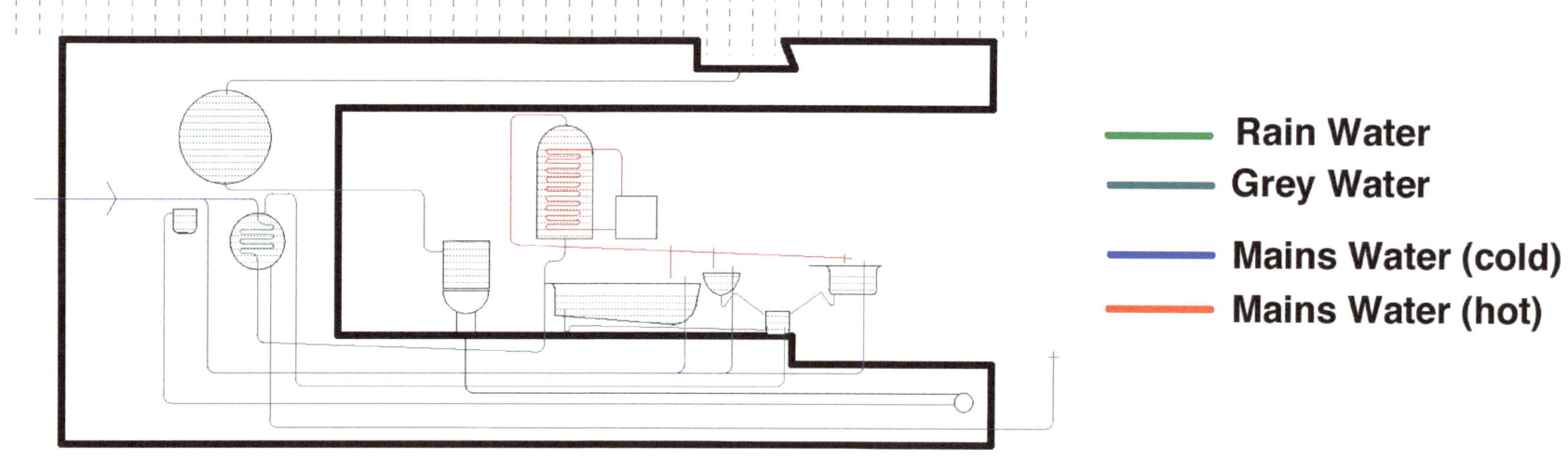

Figure 2/14. Section-diagram showing the water re-cycling system of the Pandinus House

Figure 2/15. View inside a Pandinus House looking from the main living space towards the stairway

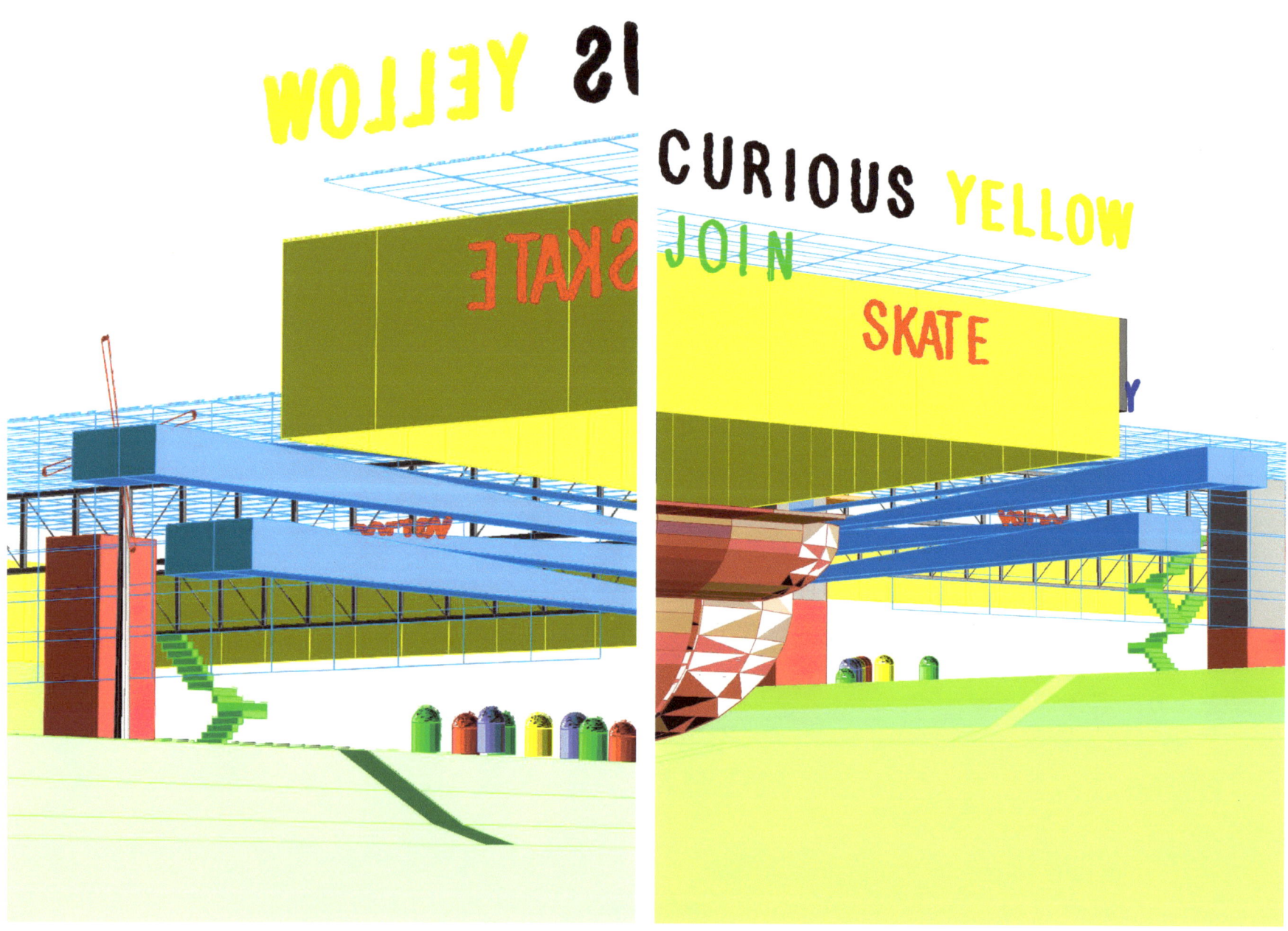

Figure 2/16. Perspective projections showing an abstract compostion of CY elements

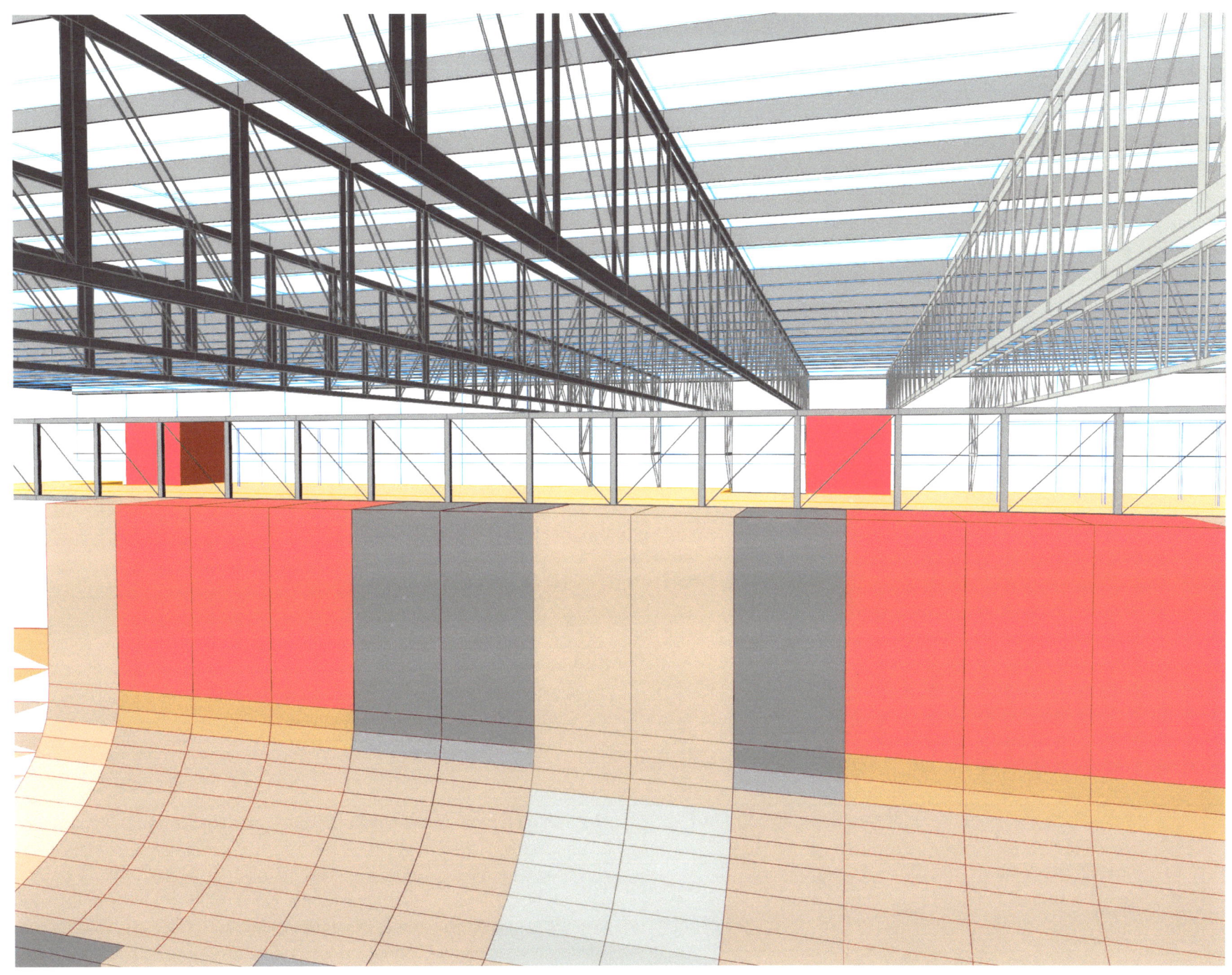

Figure 2/17. Perspective projection showing a possible CY performance space configuration

Project THREE: Concept House 2000

When considering the future of domestic architecture, entrants should consider that householders in the year 2000 are not living in outer space as widely predicted in the 1950s (Competition Brief)

From whichever sector these wide spread predictions of millennial outer spatiality were emanating, there was at least one group whose interest in space was decidedly different: in the 1950s architects were preoccupied with the immediate, terrestrial problem of mass production housing.

One example from those days was the prototype Row House, by Ludwig Mies van der Rohe.

As explained in an article published in the Architectural Forum in 1958:

Mies' row-house plan carries the concept of open planning as far as it has ever gone. It is a service core dropped on a clear slab for the buyer to subdivide as he wishes - almost the exact equivalent of the rental of open office space in a new building.

The idea is illustrated in the plan below, showing 3 Row House units.

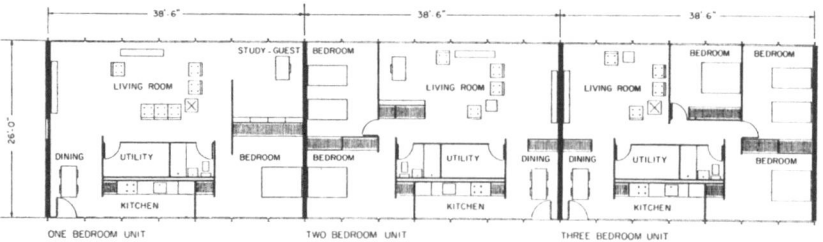

Notice how the dimensions of the slab and the location of the service core (marked 'utility') upon the slab is always the same. On the other hand, the arrangement of furniture and partitions is configured differently for each unit.

The stated equivalence between open planning in the home and in the office is interesting because it implies the place of work - the office - and the place of non-work - the home - are similar. As is well known, Mies went on to explore open planning in all his subsequent projects. For example, if we look at a typical floor plan of, say, the Toronto Dominion Centre we see it is composed of the same elements as the prototype houses: slab, core and open space awaiting subdivision.

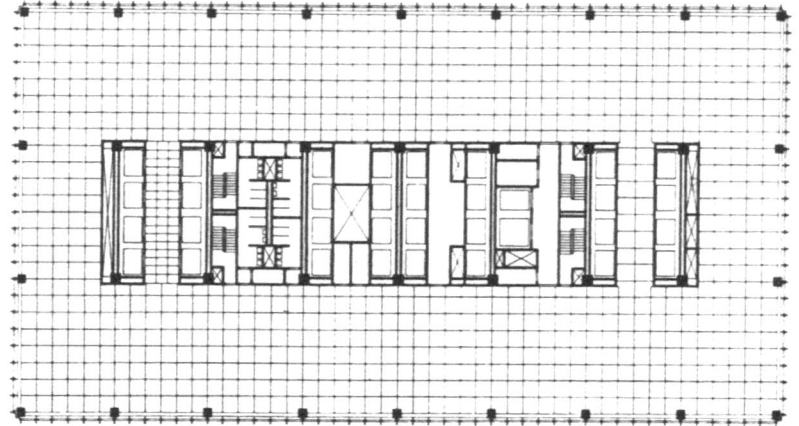

DWAs project for a prototype house for the year 2000 evolved around two themes derived from the Row House
1. freedom of the plan
2. equivalence of non-work and work

Proposal

The prime element of the Concept House is a timber frame in the shape of a house, we called this P. It serves as a basic form element that can be equipped with a range of spatial devices, such as a stair, a lift, a service (kitchen or bathroom). By equipping the basic unit P a series of qualified form types can be generated. We denote them A, B, C, D; etc., (see below). The form types can be connected together to build a house, connections can be aligned parallel to the pitch of the roof, or continuous with the pitch, we call the former 'extension' and the latter 'addition' (Figure 3/1). There is a further level of variability within the form types including the moving parts and the variable materiality of screens, blinds, partitions, and platforms. Detached and free to roam within the house and its immediate environment is a flotilla of sensors, these relay information back and forth between the exterior and the interior of the house. Their operation ranges from relaying information at a global level to the simple detection of local changes in temperature. The information thus gathered may be projected onto a screen, or interpreted as a signal to turn on the heating.

List of Form Types
A. Merely a structure; B. the most general of the form types, a glass wall enclosure, a series of external blinds, a suspended timber floor; C. the glass wall can 'open' to connect interior and exterior; D. the blinds can be extended to cover the entire external surface of the house; E. a form type that is enclosed on three sides. This form type can be used as an 'end bay'; F. a form type housing a lift; G. a form type housing a stair; H. any form type accommodating servicing elements: H/i kitchen at ground and first floor level, H/ii bathroom at ground and first floor level, H/iii bathroom at ground, kitchen at first floor level, H/iv kitchen at ground, bathroom at first floor level; J. a general form type with partitions introduced to sub-divide the space. Partitions can be at either level, or both and they can be full height or part height: J/i. part height at ground level, J/ii. full height at ground and first floor levels, J/iii. part height at ground and first floor levels, J/iv. full height at ground and part height at first floor level (Figure 3/2).

Construction
i) Structure: Vertical structural frames, at 3.6 metre centres, form the basic 'house' shape. Cross-bracing between the frames confirms the house image and provides essential lateral stability. Each frame is divided vertically by a laminated timber beam, rafters at 1.2 metre centres span between the beams and support the suspended first floor; ii) Enclosure: Glass panels are fixed onto the face of the structural frame. The panels are composite, consisting of an inner and an outer leaf, built-up as a 'sandwich' of 12mm glass, 12mm cavity, 12mm glass. The leaves are separated by a 100mm cavity zone. Aside from separating the inner and outer leaves of the panels, the cavity zone can be utilised: a) to run fibre optic cables for control systems, b) to accommodate, as necessary, support for the leaves (glass fins), c) to accommodate fixtures, as necessary, to allow the glass panels to slide; iii) Environment: A system of adjustable blinds is overlaid upon the outside face of the glass panels, covering parts of the house in a light-weight layer of fine reflective material. The system of blinds, taken together with the system of highly insulating, sliding, glass panels, provides a simple but highly flexible membrane between the inside and the outside of the house. Thus, on a hot summers day one can envision a situation in which all the blinds are down and all the panels are open and the interior of the house provides a cool and shady retreat from the heat outside. Conversely, on a cold winters day the blinds facing towards direct sunlight would be up, the panels closed and a warming solar gain would penetrate to the interior of the house.

Urban implications
As the place of work becomes the place of the home and vice versa, so the need to travel to work will diminish. Large scale transport infrastructure will become less congested and car ownership will decrease and residential areas will become more green and pleasant. The surface treatment of roadways will no longer need vast expanses of asphalt and concrete, instead urban surfaces may be finished with stone, cobbles, gravel and grass.

Prototype
For the ideal home exhibition 2000 we have selected a version of the house which approximates to a three bed family house. The house is an aggregate of four extended bays and one additional bay. The extended bays consist of two gable ends (E), one basic bay (B) and one core (H). The additional bay is of the staircase type (G), adapted to provide points of entry and exit to the house. The more secluded spaces - for sleeping and cleansing - are located on the ground floor while the shared spaces are on the first floor. For this reason the core adopted is of the type Hiii, with a kitchen at the upper level and a bathroom at the lower level (Figures 3/3, 3/4, 3/5 & 3/6).

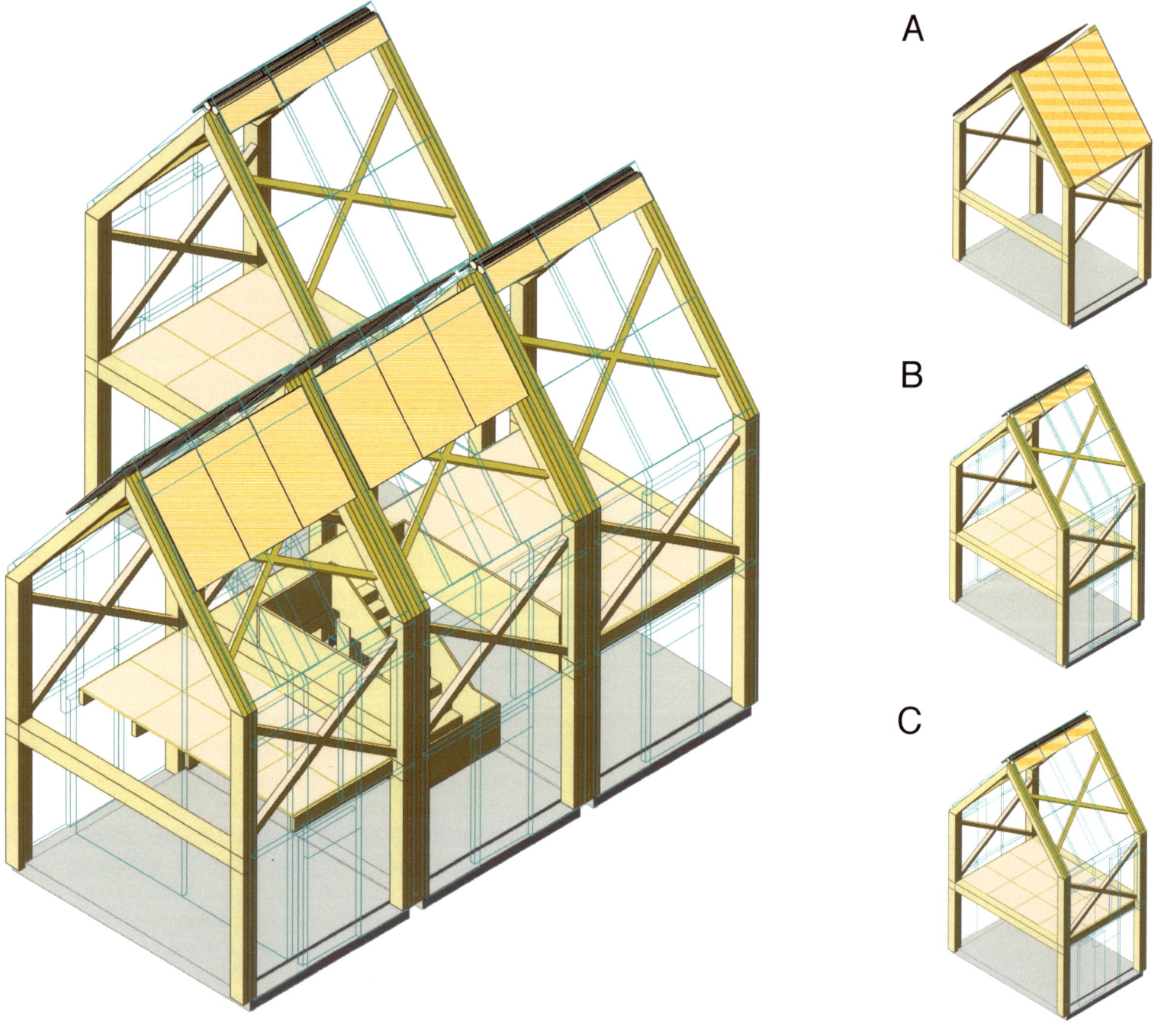

Figure 3/1. Extension & addition of Form Types

Figure 3/2. Matrix of Form Types

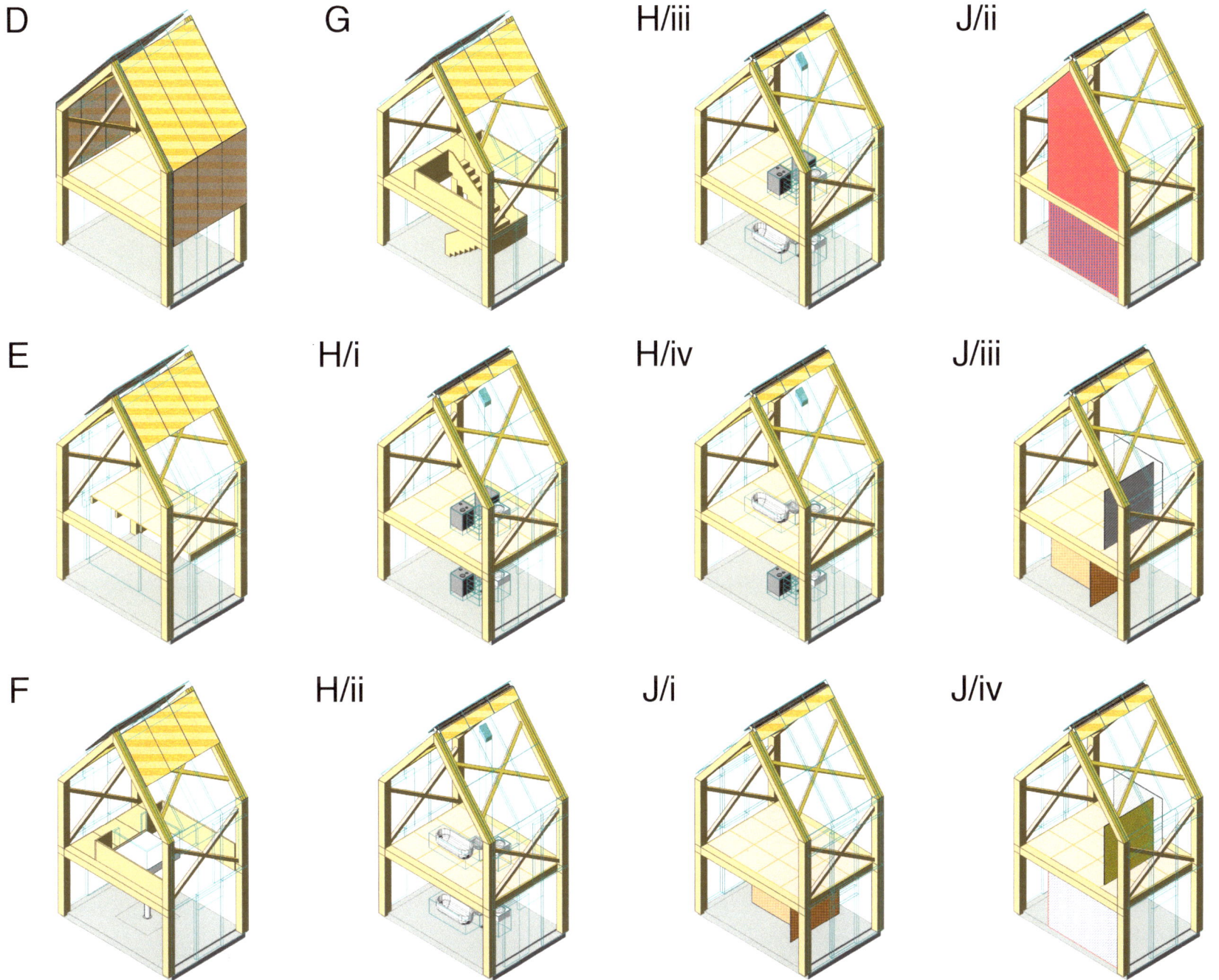

Figure 3/3. Prototype House; ground floor plan, front elevation, longitudinal section & oblique view

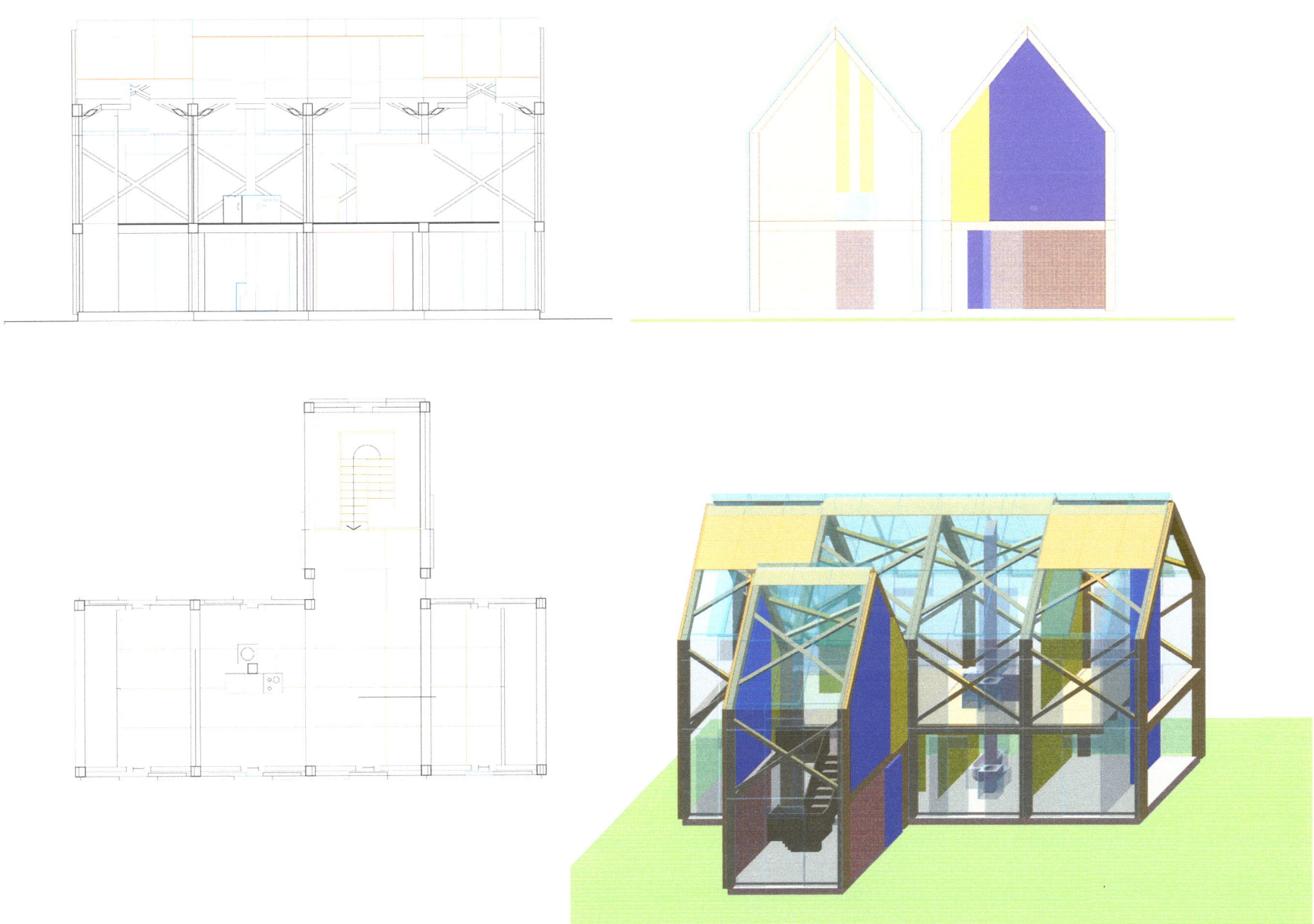

Figure 3/4. Prototype House; first floor plan, transverse section, right elevation & oblique view

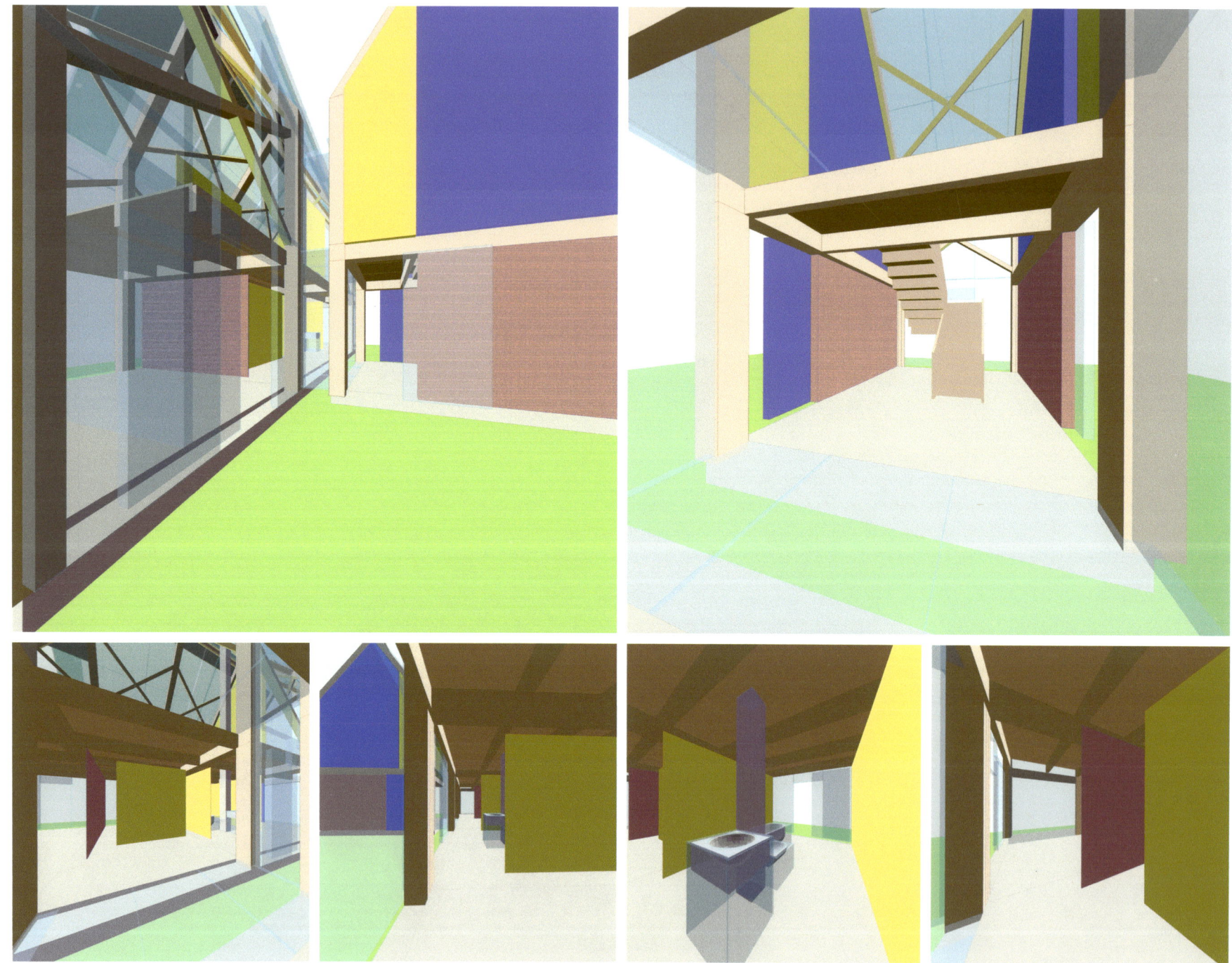

Figure 3/5. Prototype House, 6 views

Figure 3/6. Prototype House, 6 views

Project FOUR: Landmark Tower/U2 Studio

This project began as an entry for the Dublin Docklands Development Authority's concept competition for a mixed use development at Britain Quay in the Grand Dock Area in Dublin's Docklands (2003). The competition asked for an iconic tower to be 60 metres tall, which would house apartments and a penthouse recording studio for the Dublin-based pop band U2. At the time the band was enjoying a come-back with its tenth studio album *All that You Can't Leave Behind*.

What drew us to the competition was the way the competition brief and selected site already prescribed the spatial strategy, the form and the broad massing of the new building, leaving just the appearance to be determined by the designer. This did not mean the designer could simply submit an image, they had to plan the building, working hard to ensure the schedule of accommodation specified in the brief could be comfortably and efficiently distributed within their proposed building envelope.

We had just begun to work with a new material form called air grid, a three-dimensional lattice made of coloured threads held within a support frame. Although we greatly enjoyed experimenting with pure air grid structures, as it were, just for their own sake, we often asked about the possibilities of using air grid to make buildings and places. Of course we were under no illusions about the possibility of making entire buildings out of air grid since the material has no resistance to gravity and always needs an additional support, even in the pure state. But we did think it might be possible to use air grid to make space-dividing elements that would function as integral parts of the architecture of the building.

In the history of modern architecture it is well known that the invention of the elevator contributed to the development of a new type of building called the 'skyscraper.' Thanks to the elevator it became possible to abstract, replicate and multiply a single building plot into an array of identical floor-plates that could be arranged as a stack, one above the other, vertically in space. Thanks to the elevator, it was no longer necessary to move up and down a building by passing sequentially from floor-to-floor by means of a staircase, now it was possible to glide between floors, to pass some floors by and to stop at others. The invention of the elevator broke the classic order of space that understood the composition of buildings in terms of a base, a middle and a top, but it also interrupted the spatial flow. The act of using an elevator introduces an abrupt break between all floors of the building, isolating them from one another and turning each one into a spatial unit in its own right. Furthermore, in terms of experience, the elevator is a hermetic moment in a confined space and for many users of elevators the convenience of efficient vertical mobility is balanced by a claustrophobic terror that the elevator will breakdown leaving them trapped in the nowhere space between floors.

The problem with elevators is much alleviated when the shaft and the car can be made as open and transparent as possible, so the user actually gets to see the flow of space as they journey through it.

For us, the Dublin Tower competition was an opportunity to experiment with the skyscraper form and an opportunity to explore the possibilities of introducing air grid into the elevator experience. We proposed to define the elevator shaft by means of a finely woven air grid lattice and to designate each floor level with its own colour mix. We did not intend to have abrupt colour breaks between floors but to introduce a gradation of colour from top to bottom. We based our design for the elevator shaft on the spherical relations of colour as illustrated in, for example, Philip Otto Runge's Colour Sphere. Of course a lift shaft is not spherical and it was just the relations of the colours that we took for our elevator shaft design, not the shape. As you can see from the illustration on the facing page (figure 18) the shaft begins at the bottom with cyan and ends at the top with maroon. In between it passes through rose, pale orange, green, yellow, orange, ochre, dark green, blue, pink and red.

Even with animated drawings, it is impossible to capture what it would actually be like to pass through the air grid lattice. Air grid is not spectacular and these drawings can only allude to the diffuseness of the colour and the moire sensation of the grid, they cannot evoke it.

Figure 4/1. Weaving the elevator shaft

Figure 4/2. Perspective view of the Tower, approaching from the west

Figure 4/3. Perspective view of the Tower, approaching from the east

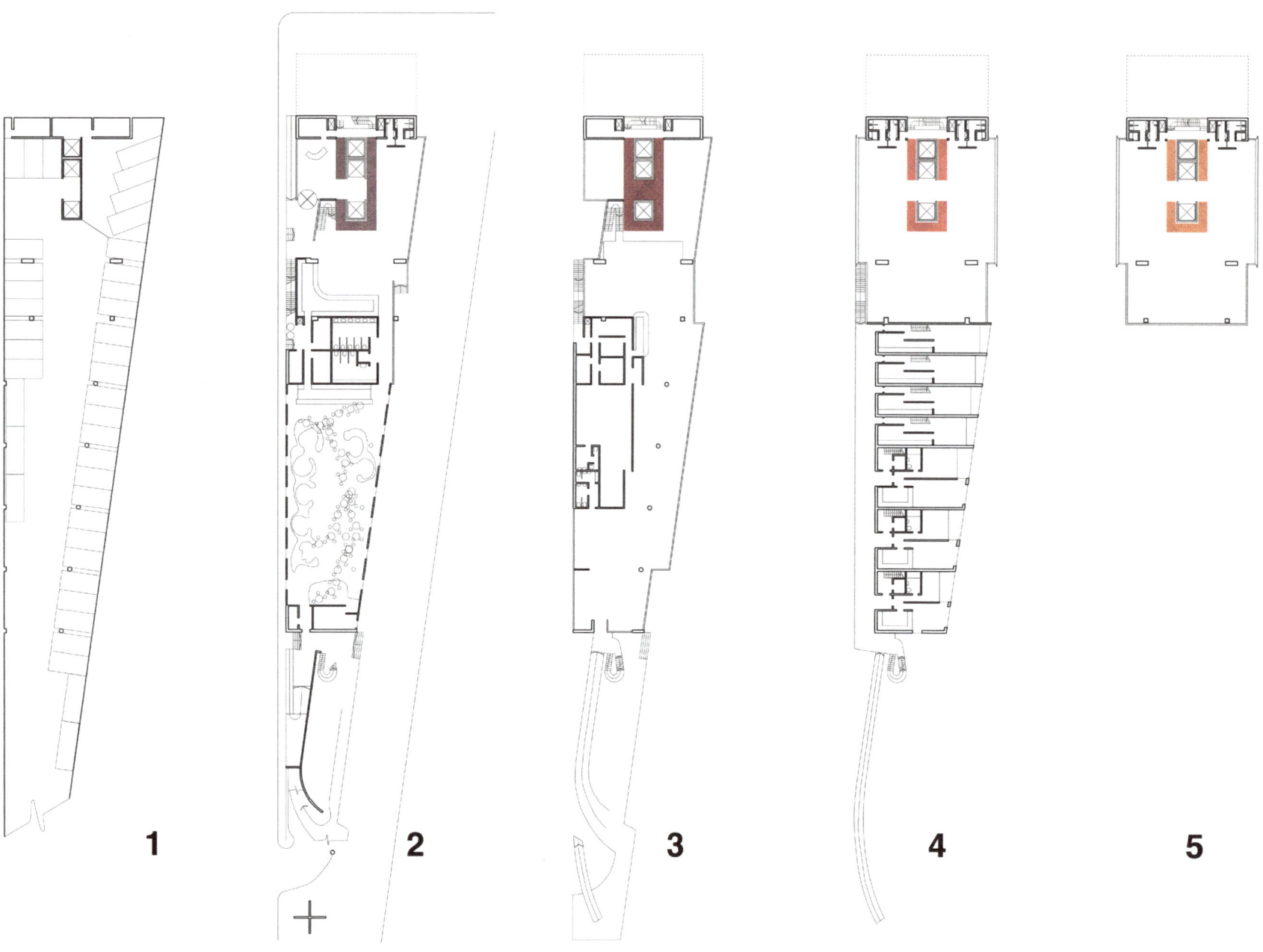

Figure 4/4. Floor plans: 1. basement; 2. ground floor; 3. mezzanine; 4. flats; 5. tower (empty floor plan)

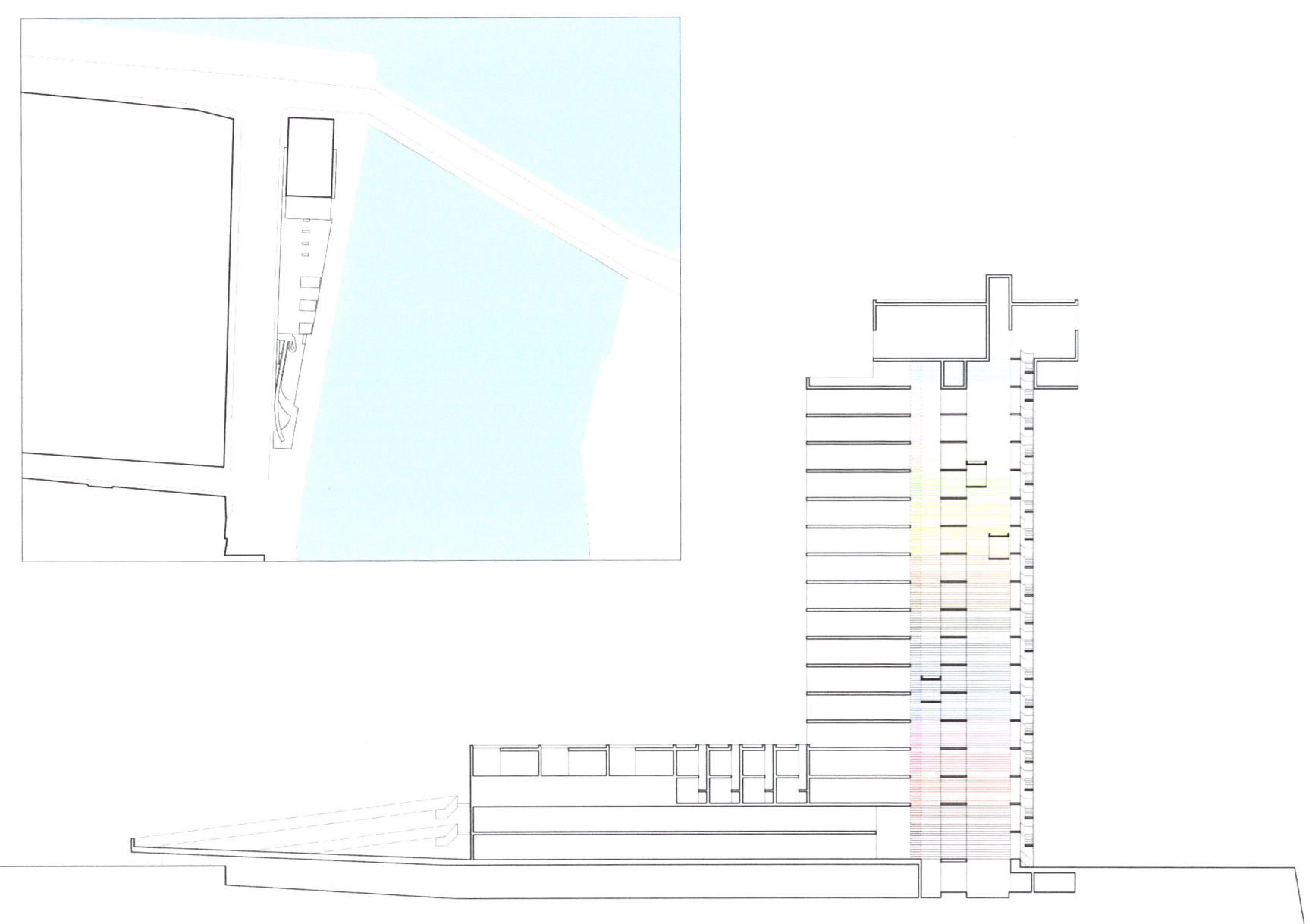

Figure 4/5. Long section (site plan inset)

Project FIVE: Salt Housing Block

This project began as an entry for a competition aimed to address the predicted need for an additional 400,000 new homes in the metropolitan region of Barcelona (2004). The competition was conceived on a territorial scale, proposing three different locations with diverse geographic peculiarities and programmatic requirements. By proposing three different scenarios the competition aimed to go beyond practical solutions and to raise questions about growth, building density and the sustainability of the very limited territory. We decided to work on the given location in the municipality of Salt.

We were attracted to the competition because it gave us the opportunity to think about architecture and the politics of everyday life. Along with most of the other entrants we took the view: the architecture of the house plays a pivotal role in shaping the politics of everyday life and cannot remain neutral in this respect. While the influence of architecture is often overlooked, it has traditionally upheld the ideology of the nuclear family as the ideal social norm in housing. However, the current housing crisis in many countries reflects a growing demand for alternative domestic arrangements based on increased individual autonomy and nontraditional groupings. In the future, residential architecture needs to embrace and articulate these developments, which have been hindered by social hierarchies and economic dependencies.

We began with a conceptual entity: *The Housing Block*
As a concept The Housing Block is intangible and transcends matter and time, as architects however, our focus lies in its material manifestation. Our project envisioned materialisation of the Block through the lens of four craftwork forms - masonry, carpentry, weaving, and pottery - these can be considered basic ingredients of any architectural structure.

Our proposal aimed to create an urban artefact that maintains architectural coherence while adapting to the needs of self-selected human groups, varying in size and organisational structures that evolve over time. The Housing Block concept facilitates the creation of spaces that are not only functional but also empowering, reflecting the values and aspirations of the inhabitants. It will serve as a catalyst for positive social change, promoting inclusivity, equality and well-being in the everyday lives of its residents.

The basic ingredients of The Housing Block are:

1. Mound: Distinguishing itself from a vehicle, a dwelling symbolises the return of the body to the protection of the earth. Similar to a child finding solace in its mother's embrace, a dwelling provides a secure place to rest. Our project proposes a mound-like structure formed through an extractive process, as if sculpted from solid rock.

2. Framework: The construction of a framework allows abstract determinations of extension and size to be translated into physical space. By utilising measurement and number, The Block enters the realm of design. We propose a framework (with spatial increments of 2.4, 3.6, and 7.2 meters) that can accommodate a wide range of available materials and technologies, reflecting common domestic habits.

3. Screens & Covers: Through intelligent and responsive systems, The Block can establish and regulate interactions with the outside world. Such interactions may encompass political, material, ambient, and sensory aspects, which we understand as expressions of material and psychophysical needs and values. The covers and screens work synergistically with ambient factors, adapting and transforming energies and potentials rather than excluding or denying them.

4. Hearth: The most intangible aspect of The Block, the hearth is intimately connected to the household, manifesting as an affective quality rather than a spatial volume, material form, or technological artefact. The hearth mirrors the real-world presence of the people who constitute the household and the place they call home. It emanates from the collective and absorbs them, fostering mutual recognition, sharing, decision-making, responsibility, and trust.

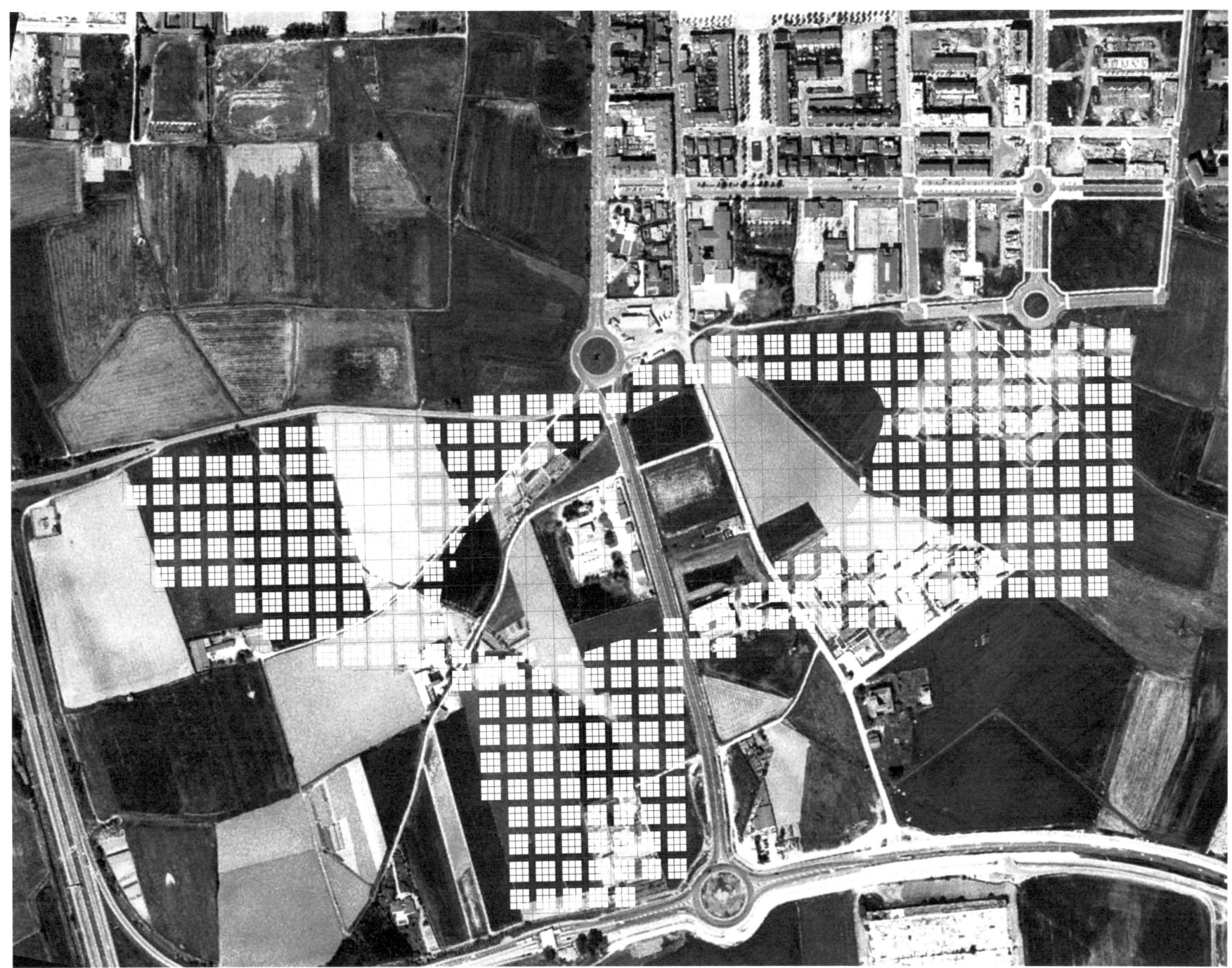
Figure 5/1. Site plan, an aggregate of Housing Blocks laid out on a grid pattern with a large open space carved out at the centre

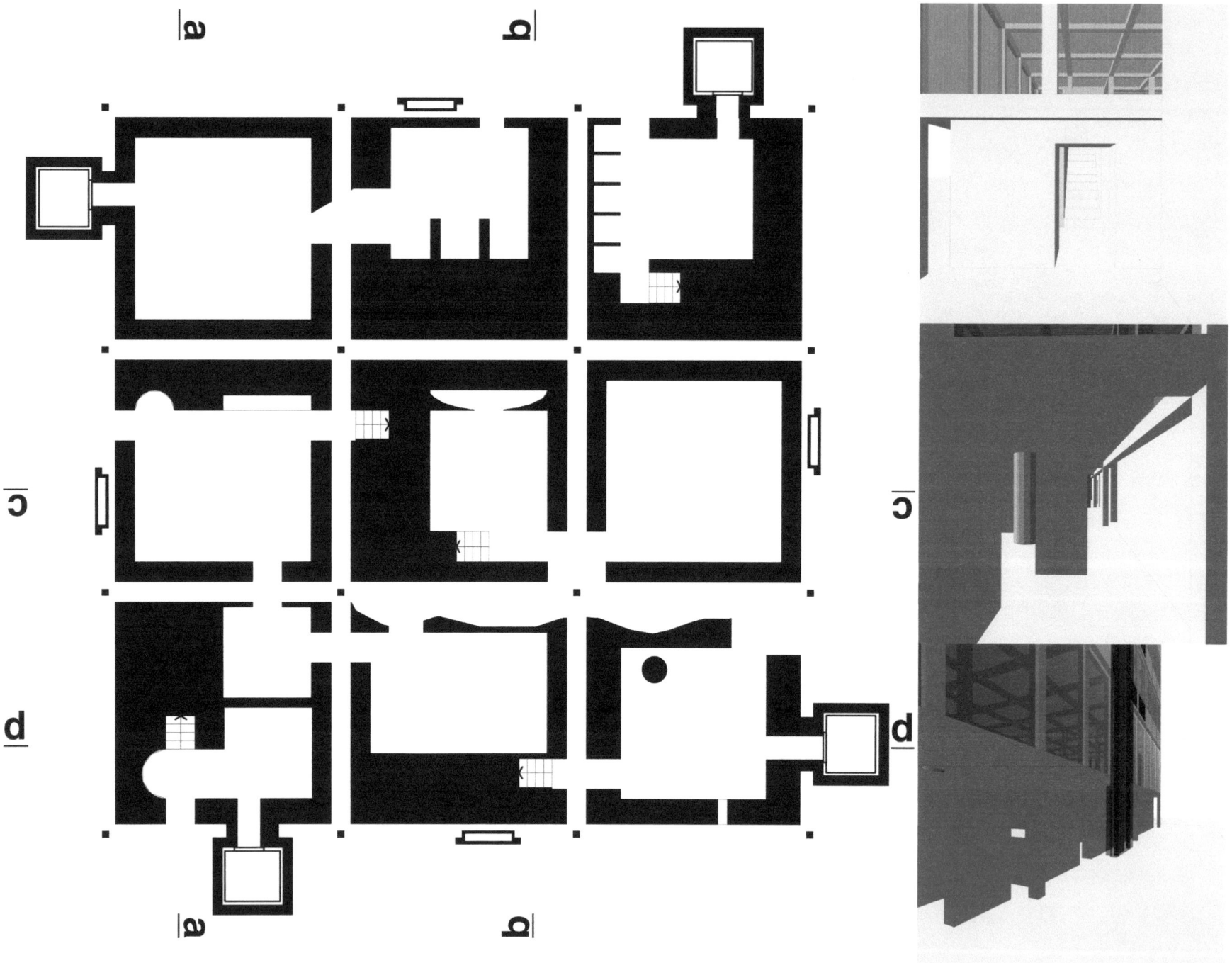

Figure 5/2. Housing Block, ground floor plan with 3 selected views at this level

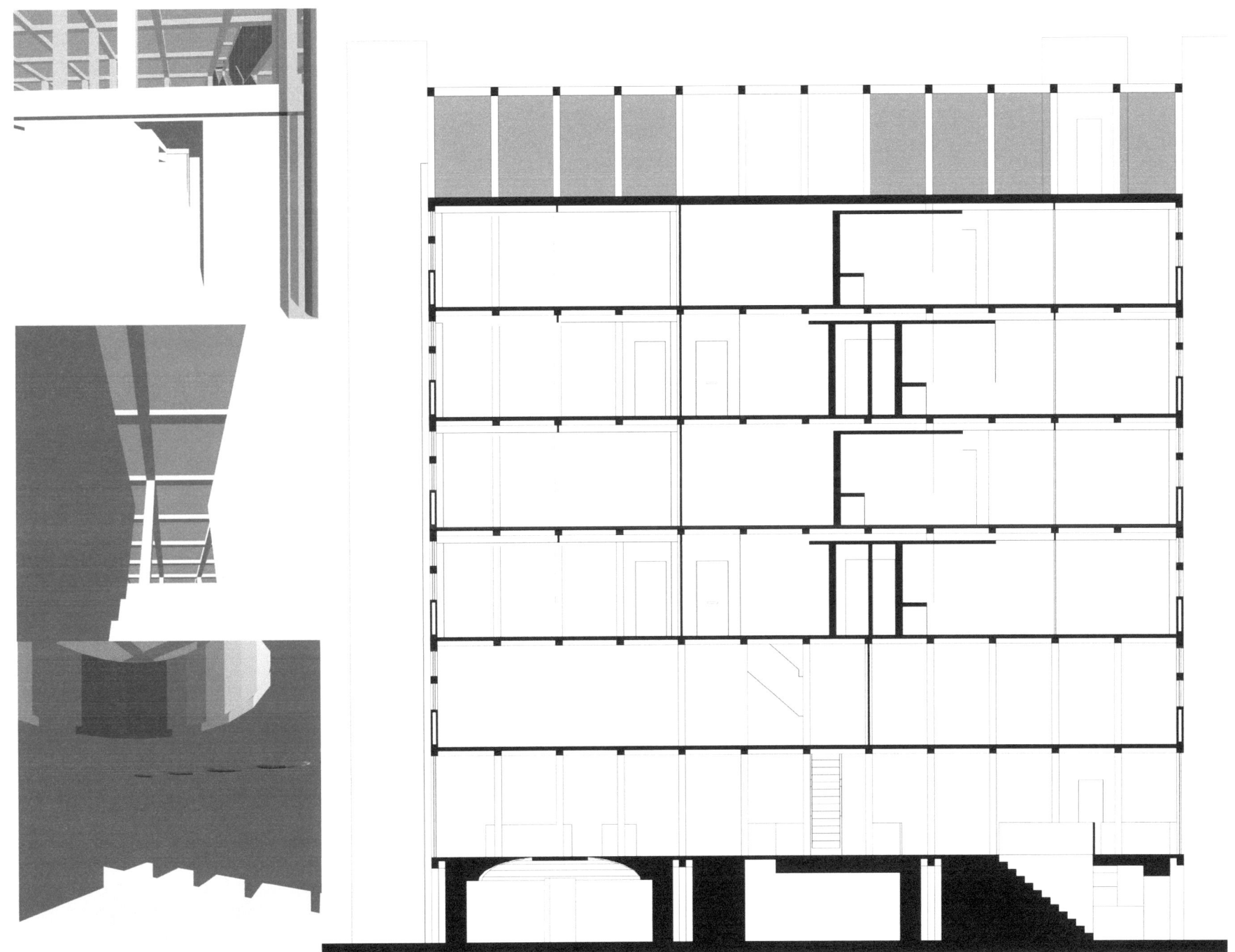

Figure 5/3. Housing Block, 3 selected views at ground floor level and section aa

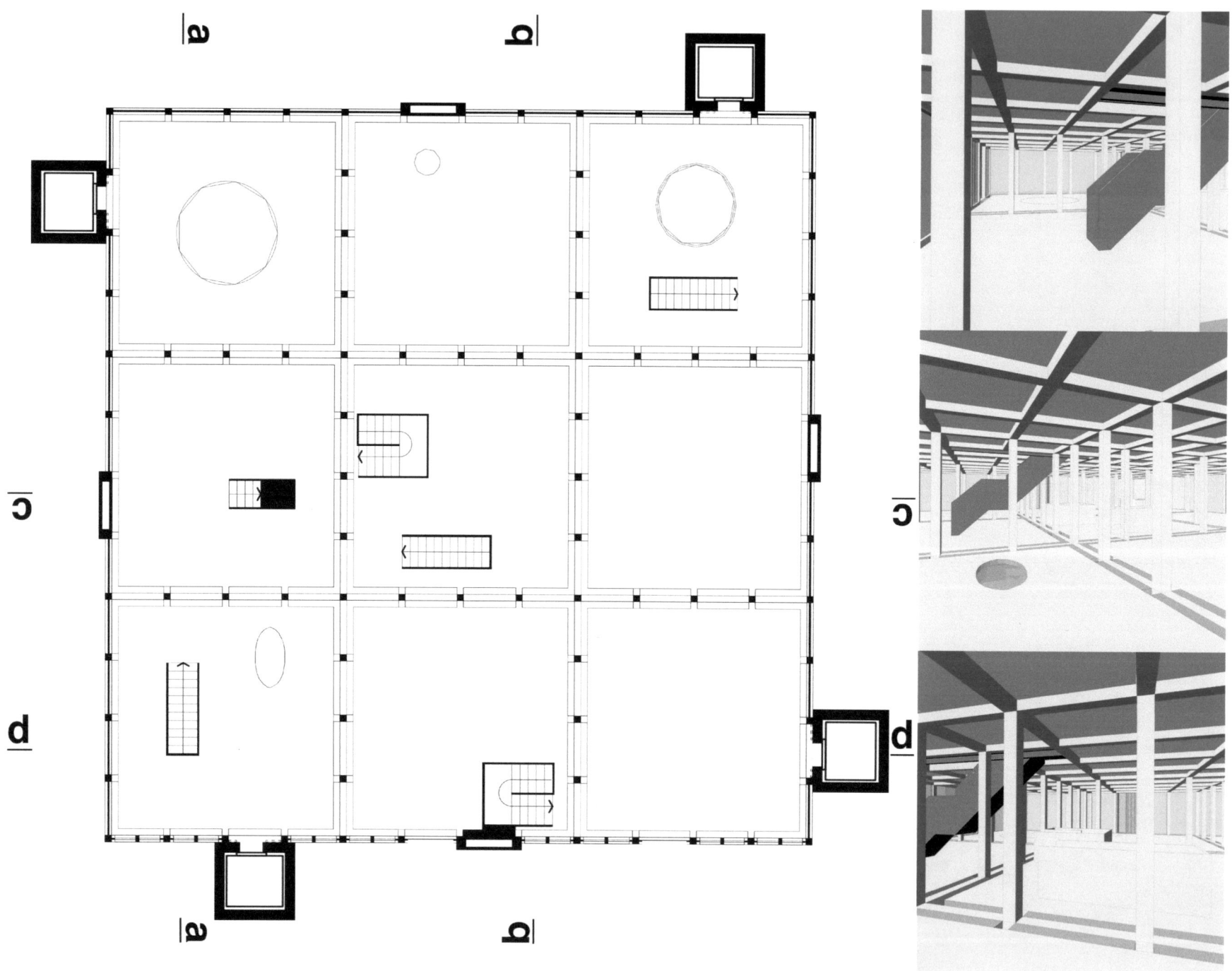

Figure 5/4. Housing Block, mezzanine floor plan with 3 selected views at this level

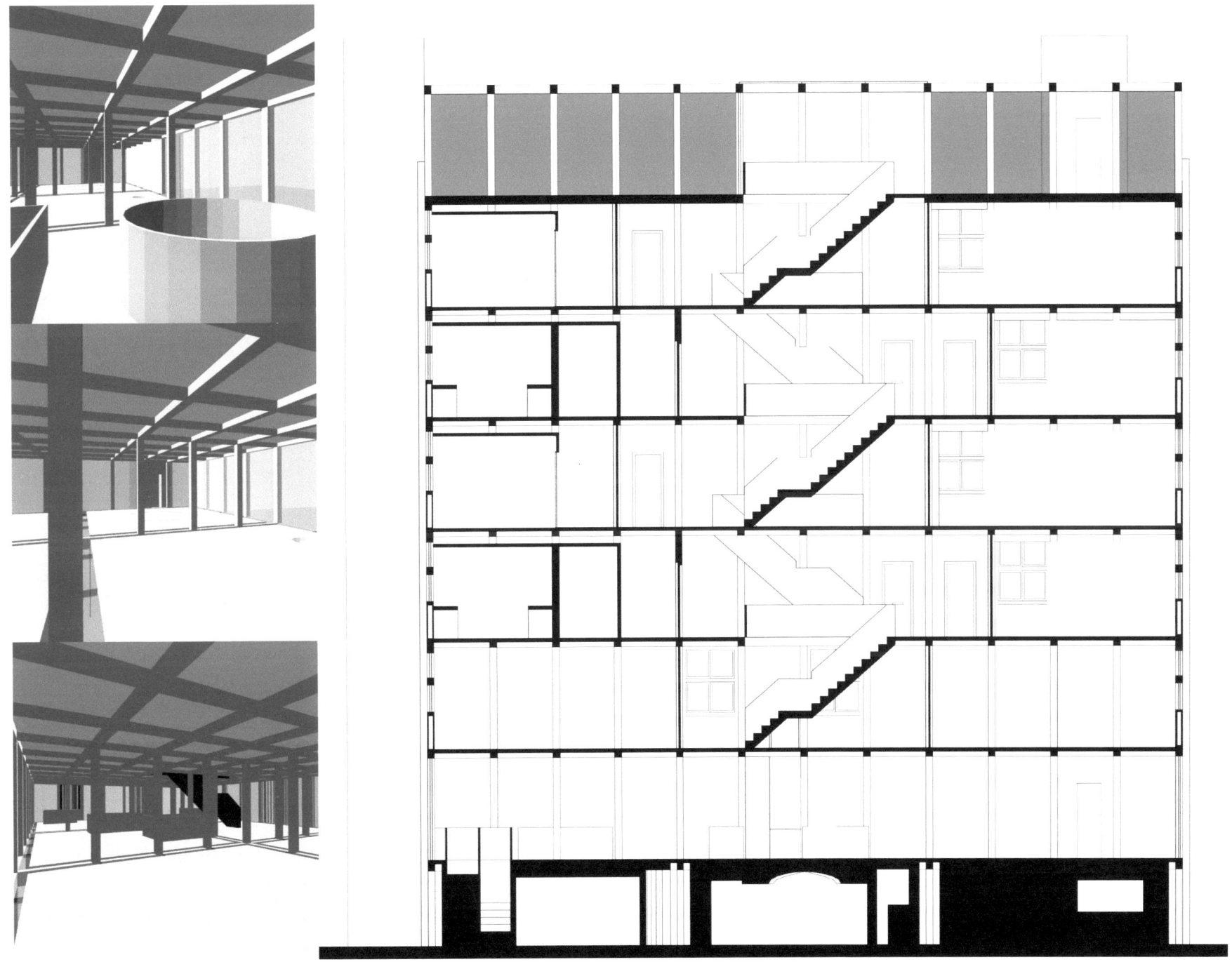

Figure 5/5. Housing Block, 3 selected views at mezzanine floor level and section bb

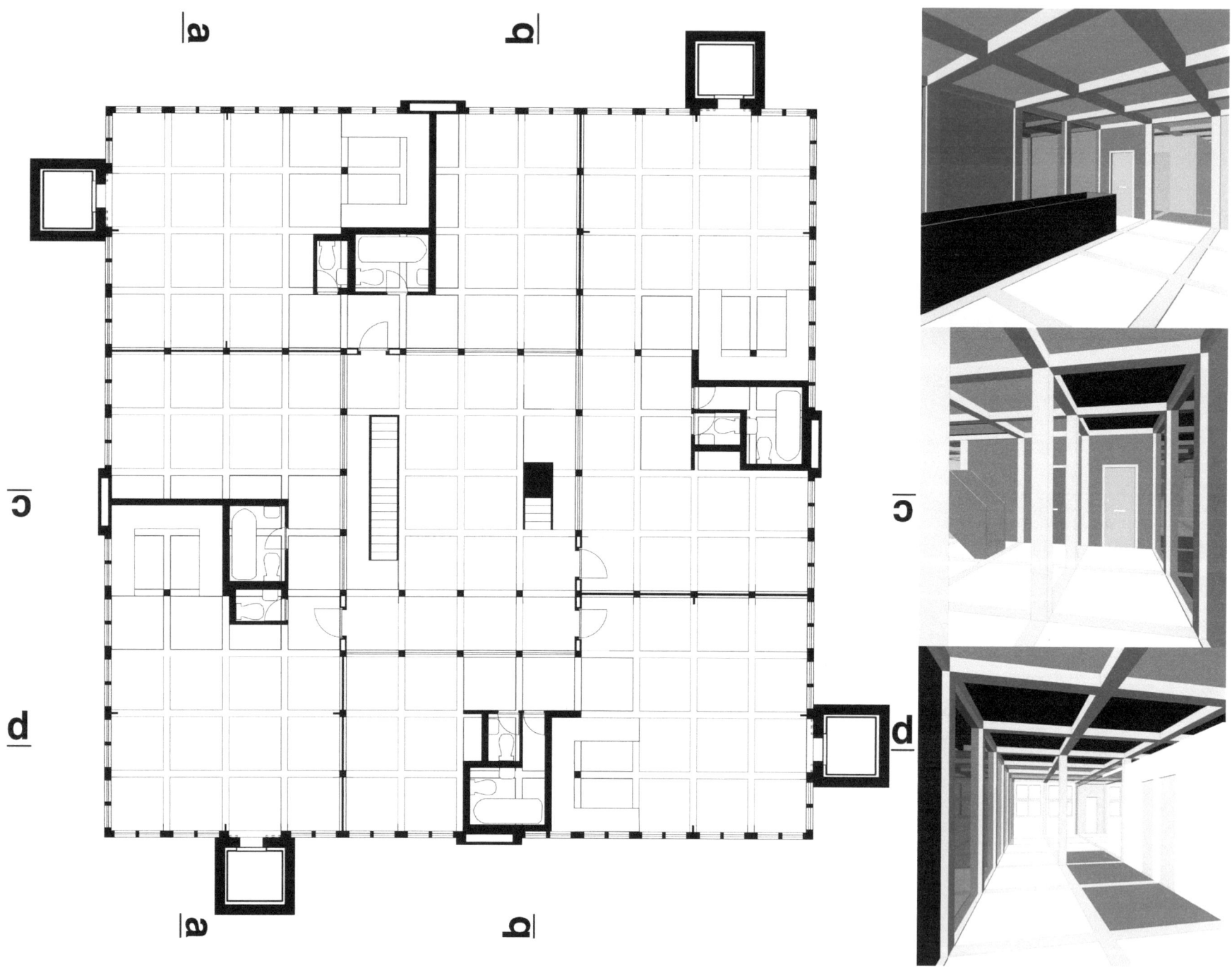

Figure 5/6. Housing Block, example of a possible floor plan, subdivided into four dwellings, with 3 typical views

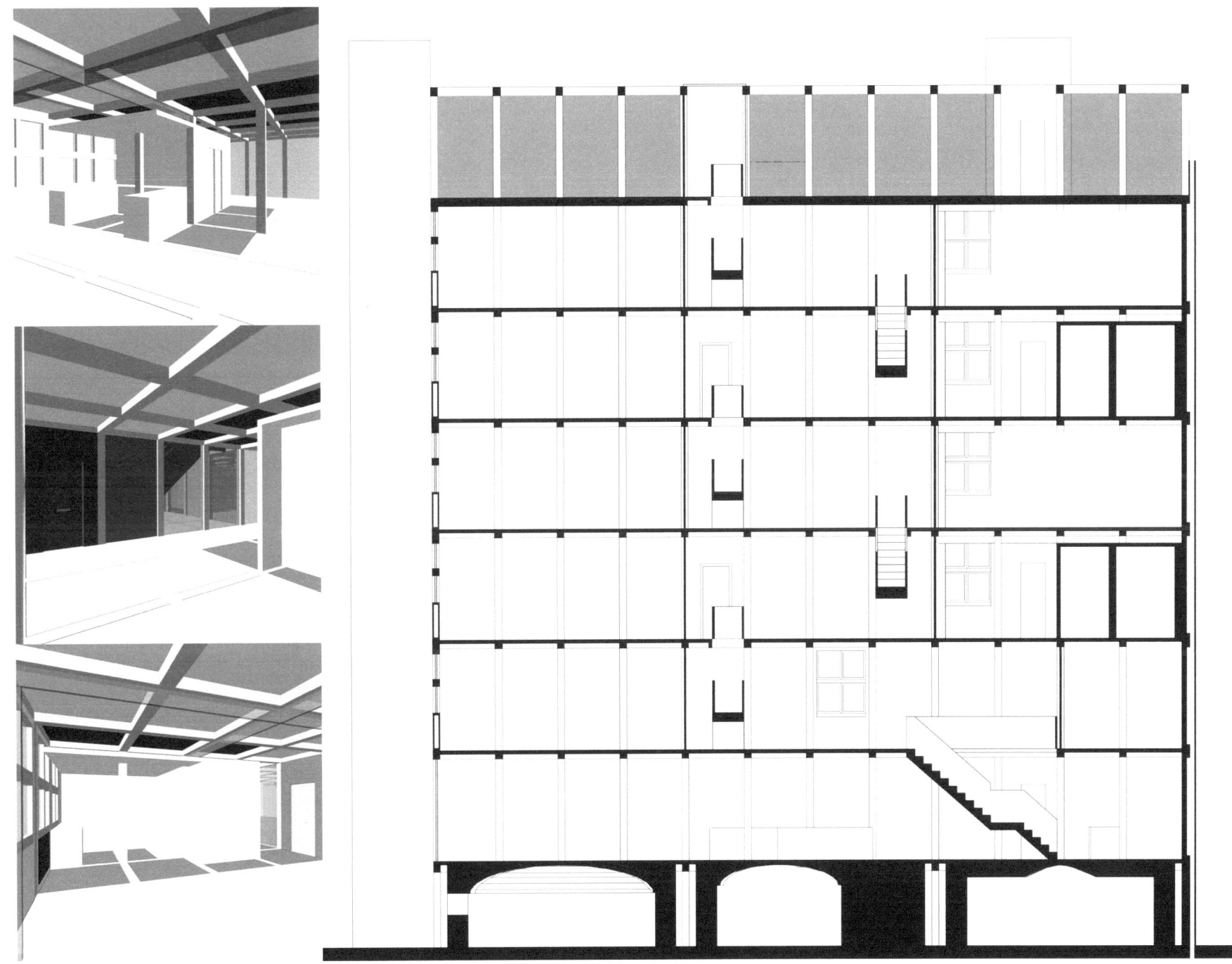

Figure 5/7. Housing Block, 3 typical views, related to the plan shown on the opposite page and section cc

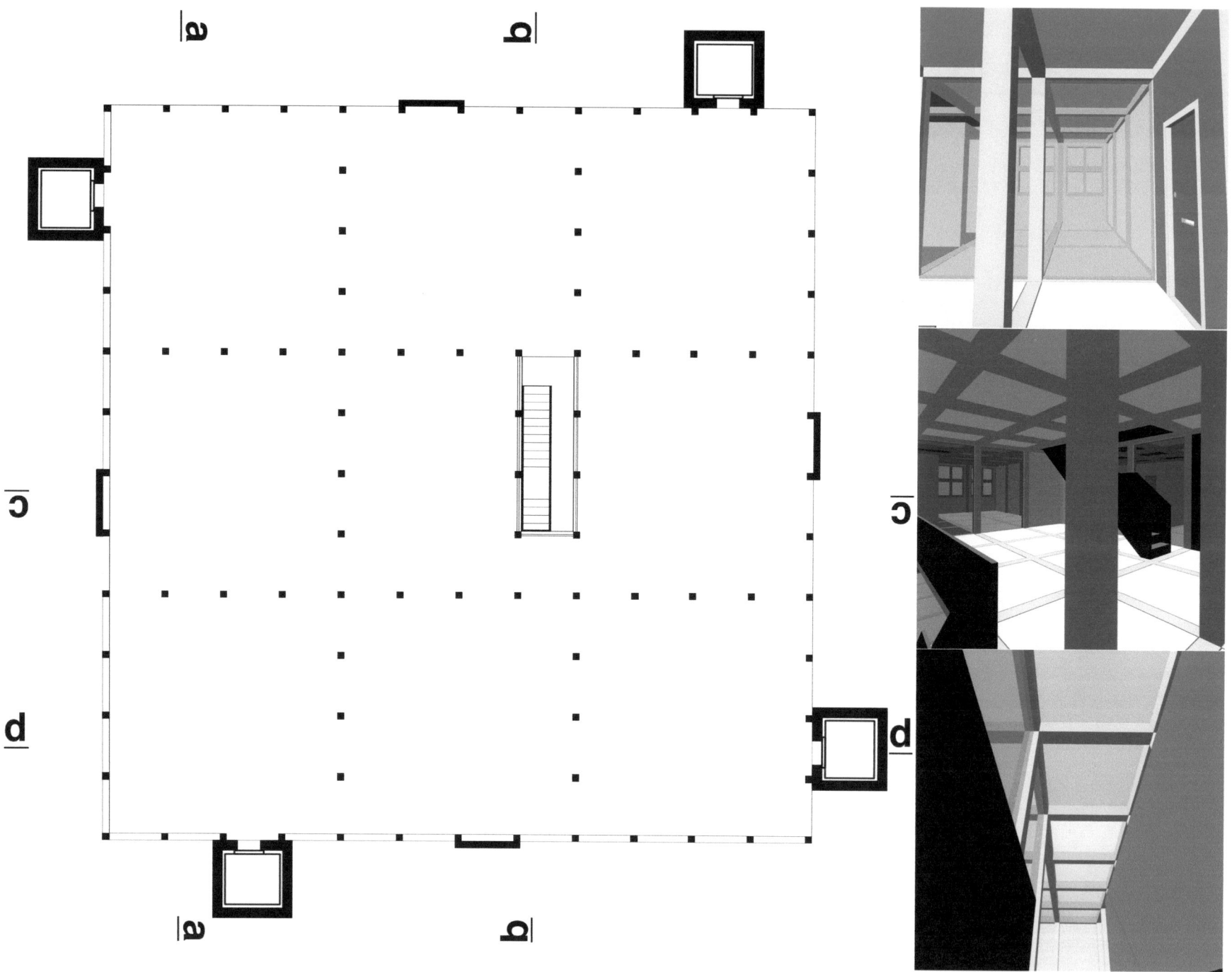

Figure 5/8. Housing Block, roof level floor plan with 3 typical views

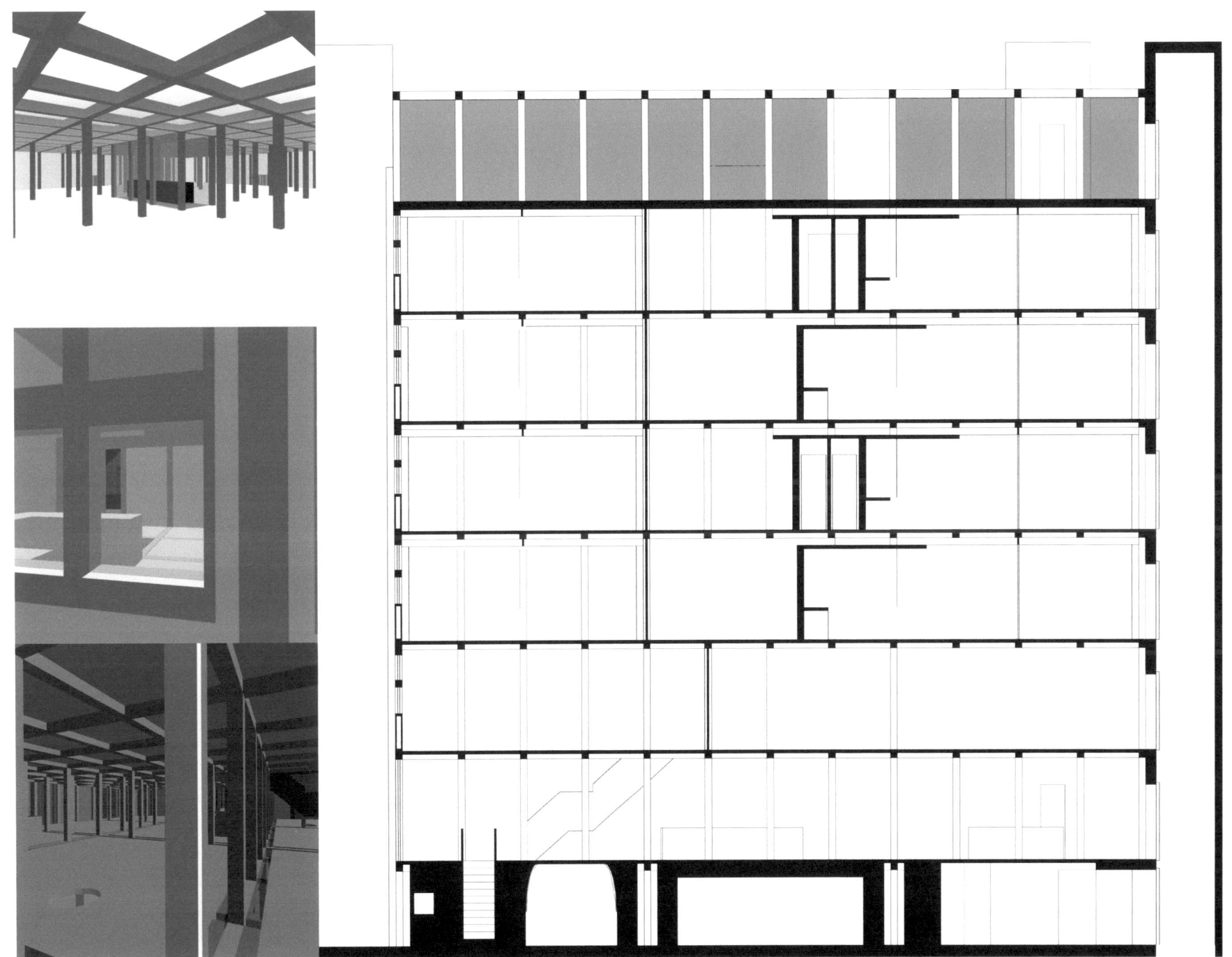

Figure 5/9. Housing Block, 3 typical views at roof level and section dd

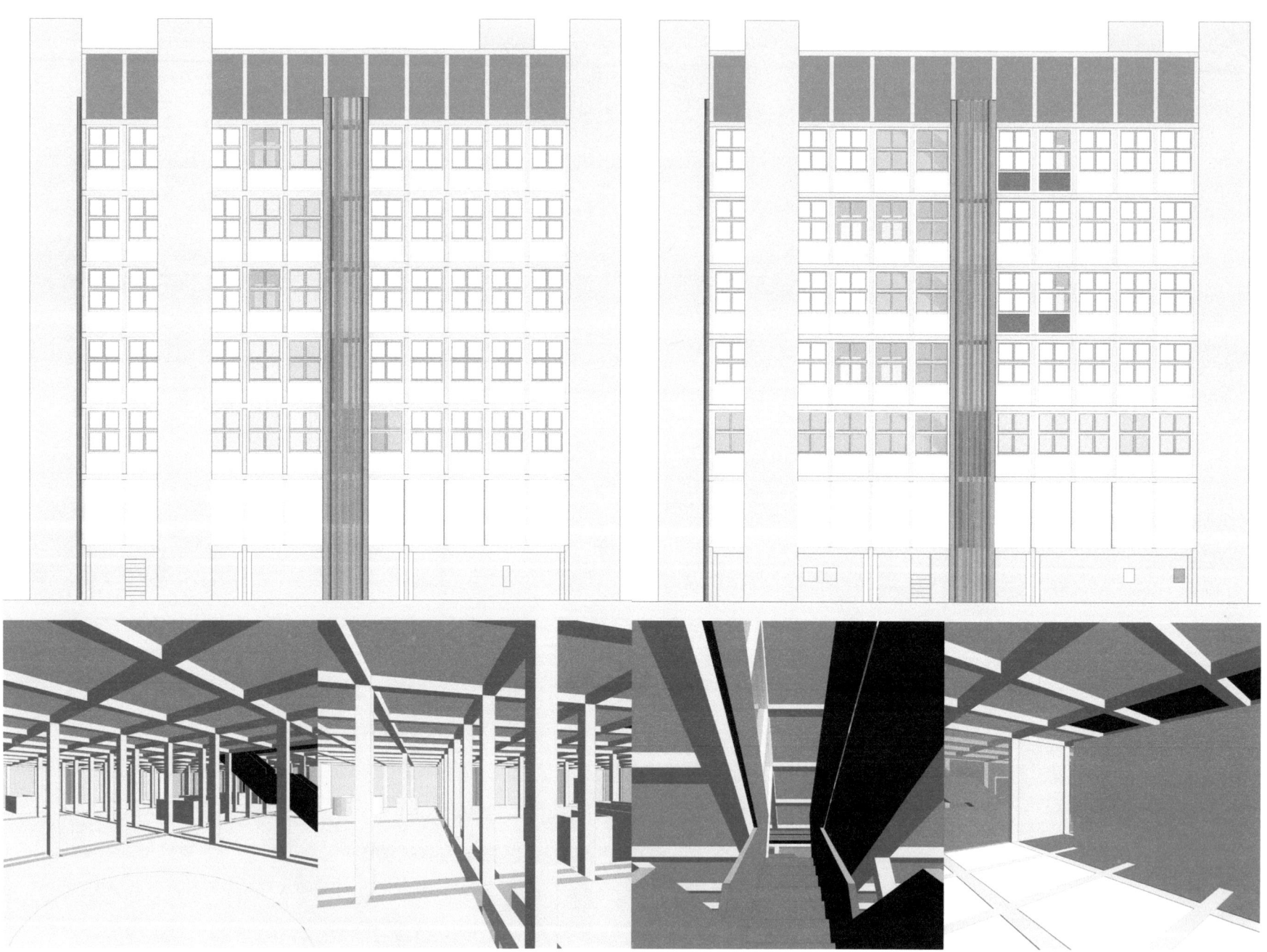

Figure 5/10. Housing Block, front and left elevations with 4 interior views at various levels

Figure 5/11. Housing Block, back and right elevations with 4 interior views at various levels

Project SIX: Lunar Leap

This project began as a response to an open design competition from 2004 that asked for designs for a pavilion to sit at the foot of Coney Island's notorious Parachute Jump. But at the time we were preoccupied with Yves Klein's Architecture of the Air and as we worked on the project the interest in Klein took over and we found ourselves departing from the aims of the competition brief. The final form taken by the project was that of an illustrated lecture and we have set it out here following the lecture format, with the text first followed by key images of the slideshow presentation.

Musing on Air
Think of the Blue of the Sky (figure 6/1). There is a good scientific explanation for why the sky is blue, the sky is blue because light with a short wavelength – for example blue light with a wavelength of 450 nanometres – is more likely to be scattered by an air particle than is light with a longer wavelength – for example red light with a wavelength of 600 nanometres. So the reason the sky is blue is because it is full of blue photons bouncing too and fro between particles of air.

However, the scientific explanation for why the sky is blue does not account for the specific quality of blueness that is the characteristic appearance of the sky as seen with human eyes. The blue of the sky appears as a nebulous, translucent species of blue, it looks insubstantial, as if it were a pure colour without body. The technical term for colours that are like the blue of the sky is *film colour*.

Yves Klein is best known for his monochrome paintings, which he painted with a special paint, invented by himself and named International Klein Blue (figure 6/2). In fact Klein did not only paint in monochrome IKB but also in monochrome Pink and monochrome Gold. The three colours together form a unique colour world that gives to Klein's work a strong sense of unity. Klein's ambition for his paintings was to bind pigment as loosely as possible to the surface of the canvas, this is why his paintings look powdery – and of course they make a special contribution to the project of free colour.

Klein is also known for this fantastic work of staging, this is a picture of himself leaping from a building and appearing to fly through the air, the picture was captioned: The Painter of Space Leaps into the Void (figure 6/3).

DWA became interested in Yves Klein's proposal for The Architecture of the Air. The essential ingredient of Klein's Air Architecture is the idea of a roof, consisting of a covering of compressed air, which would give direct visual access to the sky. The air roof would form a climatic barrier, sheltering places for human habitation without enclosing them, the idea was that it could be deployed at various scales ranging from a house, an urban district to sheltering a whole city (figure 6/4).

Klein's proposal for the Architecture of the Air got DWA thinking about air and about colour. We knew it was wrong of Klein to equate air with the void of space, but at the same time we ourselves had no idea of the manner in which Earth's atmosphere ceases to be air and dissipates into the void of space?

In order to help us think we made a large scale cross-section through the air (figure 6/5), in doing so we found out, only a tiny portion of the atmosphere, a zone, in the order of five miles high, ascending from the surface of the Earth and named the troposphere is breathable and subject to weather, for the rest of the atmospheric extent things are entirely different.

As we were thinking about colour and air we began work on our project for the open design competition mentioned above. The Lunar Leap was our response to that competition. The brief asked participants to design a pavilion to sit at the foot of the now unused Parachute Jump; a 262 foot tower of lattice ironwork from which intrepid pleasure seekers would drop, 250 feet, in seats made for two. The Jump was closed in 1968 amid safety concerns but the tower remains, it is now a city landmark. The ambition of the Lunar Leap was to create a pavilion that not only satisfies the programmatic requirements of the competition but also offers a place in the city where citizens and visitors can celebrate leaping into the air (figure 6/6).

Figure 6/1. 'Think of the blue of the sky'

Design Parameters and Narrative

The primary constructional element of our design is a cruciform gantry, held twenty feet above the ground by six, steel columns (figure 6/7). Since we wanted the gantry to appear like an object from a Suprematist painting, as if it floated above the ground, we designed the six columns to be as slender as possible, pushing them to the limits of believability.

The gantry had three purposes:

1. Roofs and upper floors are suspended from it
2. Services are accommodated in it
3. Transformable glass screens are suspended from it and it houses the mechanisms by which the screens between the restaurant, the event space and the external event area can be withdrawn and stacked clear of the opening.

The restaurant, the bar and the event space are arranged so they may be used independently, or in any combination according to the demands of particular user groups.

Servant spaces of the pavilion are contained in an earthbound component whose external form is clothed in a densely packed cage filled with plants and shrubs (figures 6/8 & 6/9).

Although the pavilion is designed to accommodate a variety of uses its primary role is to stage an event, it is this event from which the pavilion takes its name. In order to facilitate the event the gantry incorporates a special device.

Those faces of the gantry that look towards the external event area and the parachute tower are equipped with an array of four hundred and ninety six nozzles, from which jets of coloured and compressed air can be projected as vectors. The organisation of the nozzles is such that the vectors will form a colourful grid of air, just above the head height of the visitors assembled in the outdoor event space.

The Lunar Leap occurs once a month, at full moon, it unfolds as follows:

Visitors to the pavilion gather in the outdoor events space, below the gantry, the Air Grid is switched off and the visitors gaze upward toward the summit of the parachute tower, spread against the deep blue ground of the night sky. The tower will be painted a glowing, translucent white - in the daytime it will almost disappear - but at night, under the illumination of the full moon (or, in adverse weather conditions - the artificial illumination of a Moon Balloon) it will appear as a geometrical web of glowing white lines. As the visitors gaze up towards the summit of the tower so a flotilla of tiny bodies is seen to leap from the summit, gracefully they drop through the night air, limbs spread wide, they embrace the exhilaration of the free-fall (figure 6/10).

As the visitors watch, the bodies seem to grow bigger as they plummet towards them and the visitors become agitated, they are half thrilled and half dismayed in anticipation of the descending bodies impending impact (figure 6/11). But just as they reach the peak of emotional tension so, with an enormous roar, the Air Grid comes to life and jets of coloured air shoot out from the array of nozzles embedded in the gantry. The Air Grid forms a multilayered net of coloured gas in the air just above the visitor's heads. The web of coloured gas is a little misty and translucent, serving to blur what the visitors see (figure 6/12).

Although rushing closer, the falling bodies are now much harder to discern, obscured as they are by the optical vapours of the colourful grid. As the rush of gravity hurls the bodies into the grid of coloured gas, it seems to the viewers, looking up tense and anxious from below, the bodies have vanished in a puff of smoke. For the visitors it seems the impact of the falling bodies upon the Air Grid has given rise to little more than a colourful turbulence of minor shock waves.

The intense emotional thrill of the leap is dissipated, diffused into the soft lattice of coloured gas. The visitors too begin to disperse, they leave the event knowing they can never be sure if the performance was real, just an illusion or a mixture of both.

Figure 6/2. 'International Klein Blue'   Figure 6/3. 'leaping from a building and appearing to fly through the air'

Figure 6/4. 'a climatic barrier, sheltering places for human habitation'

Figure 6/5. 'a large scale cross-section through the air'

Figure 6/6. 'citizens and visitors can celebrate leaping into the air'

Figure 6/7. 'a cruciform gantry, held twenty feet above the ground'

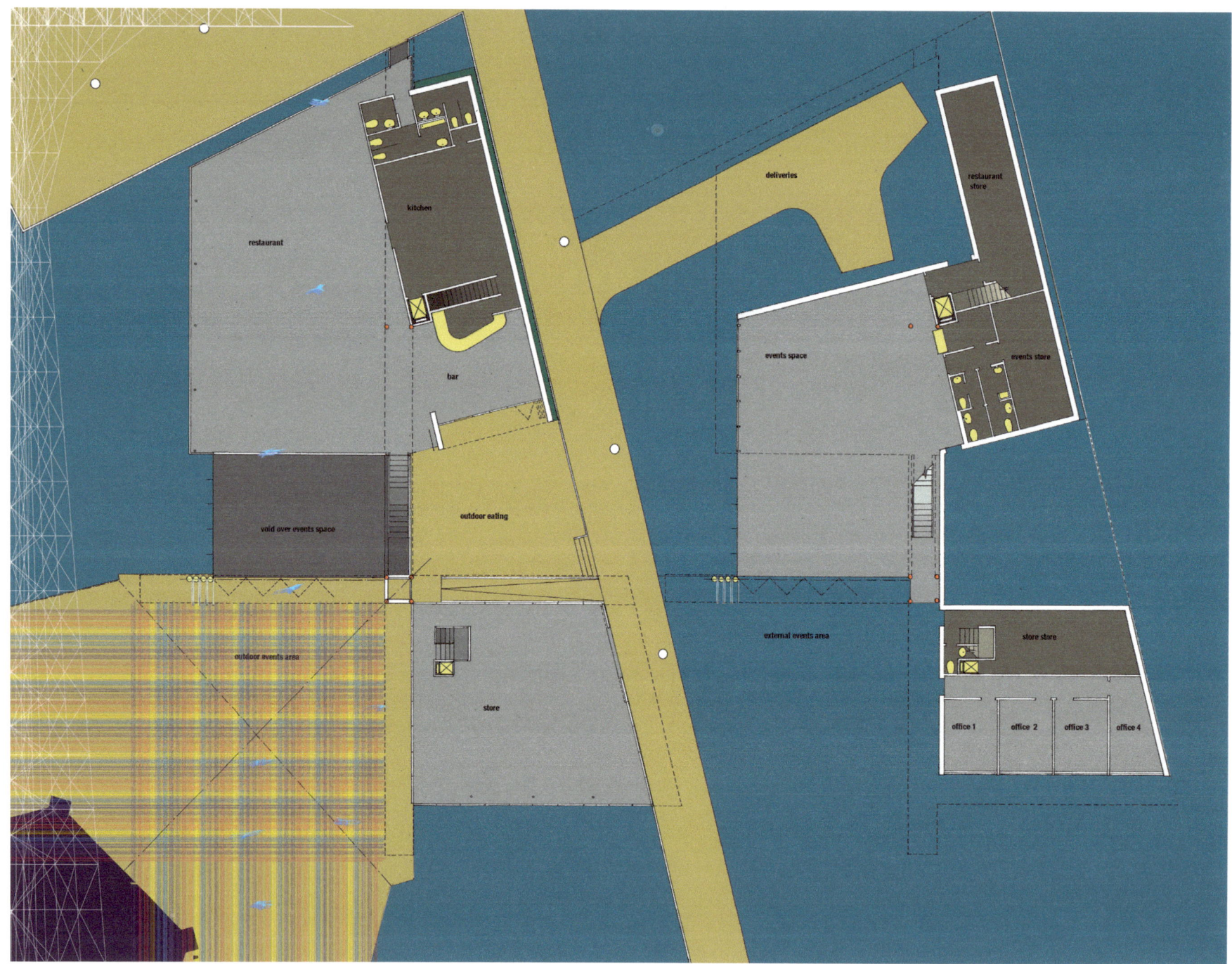

Figure 6/8. Upper and lower floor plans of the pavilion (with outline of paracute jump and falling figures)

Figure 6/9. Section through the pavilion

Figure 6/10. 'a flotilla of tiny bodies is seen to leap from the summit'

Figure 6/11. 'jets of coloured air shoot out from the array of nozzles embedded in the gantry'

Figure 6/12. 'The web of coloured gas is a little misty and translucent, serving to blur what the visitors see'

Project SEVEN: A New Skyscraper Concept

This project began as a response to an open design competition sometime around 2005, but it took on a new life as a general proposal for a new kind of skyscraper made out of artificial life-forms - we called them switch beetles - mixed in with sunlight and air.

Switch Beetles

We invented the Switch Beetles because we wanted to do something that is good for the air, not only because we are grateful to air for the maintenance of life on earth but also because air is beautiful in its own right. For both these reasons it is important to keep the air from becoming corrupted, in other words to keep it pure.

If you look carefully at the image in the middle and at the top of the opposite page (figure 7/1) you will see the Switch Beetles, they are swarming around a flash gap detail, in fact you wouldn't really be able to see them like this because they are ever so much smaller than they are drawn here, but just because human eyes can't see Switch Beetles doesn't mean they are not there.

The Switch Beetles are tiny robots, they were designed at DWA's Metaphysical Laboratories in Stevenage (figure 7/2) and they are pollution sensitive in a highly positive sense. The primary function of the Switch Beetle is to eat pollutants and the table shown on page 69 (figure 7/3) lists the specific appetites of each member of the Switch Beetle family. In fact there are 14 species of Switch Beetle and each one has its preferred menu of air pollutants that it will feed off.

The Switch Beetle combines a fowl appetite and ferocious digestive system with extraordinary beauty. A swarm of Switch Beetles can attack and gradually eat its way through a volume of polluted air (figure 7/4). But Switch Beetle activity does not stop there, having eaten up all the pollutants and so satiated their appetites the Beetles are programmed to change their behaviour. It is in the alternative mode that the Beetles become visible to the human eye.

During the eating phase the movement of the beetle swarm, if we could see it, would appear as a random pattern of colour and form. In the switched condition the Beetle movement begins to manifest a much more regular pattern. The switched condition is expressed as a slow, even movement.

In fact, if the human eye could register things that small, it would see each beetle is resting its tiny body on the waves of energy emanating from the Earth's Magnetic Field, rocking from East to West and then from North to South, the gentle movement helps their digestive processes.

As the beetles rock back and forth, so their collective body traces a lattice pattern in the air and, thanks to the architecture of the beetle body, the pattern will eventually become visible to the human eye, appearing as a loosely bound body, vibrating in response to a regular rhythm (figures 7/4 & 7/5).

Like many insects, the body of the Switch Beetle is screened by a microscopic diffraction grating and that has the effect of reinforcing the intensity of coloured light, making it almost seem as if it is a solid beam of pure colour (figure 7/1).

As the beetles rock gently back and forth, so their tiny bodies diffract the ambient light and vectors of spectral colour will appear to be amassing within the interstices of the air.

The Skyscraper

The Switch Beetles' gentle rocking becomes visible to the human eye as a vast lattice of vibrant colour, an immaterial structure, reaching up into the sky and forming a skyscraper that looks as though it hums. To the human eye the Air Grid skyscraper appears as a beautiful phenomenon, like a rainbow and the colourful form signals to the human observers that the air is now clean. In receiving the message from the Beetles it is the turn of the human observers to switch, a mood of anticipation lights up within them, just like the clear sky and feeling of freshness experienced after a fierce summer storm.

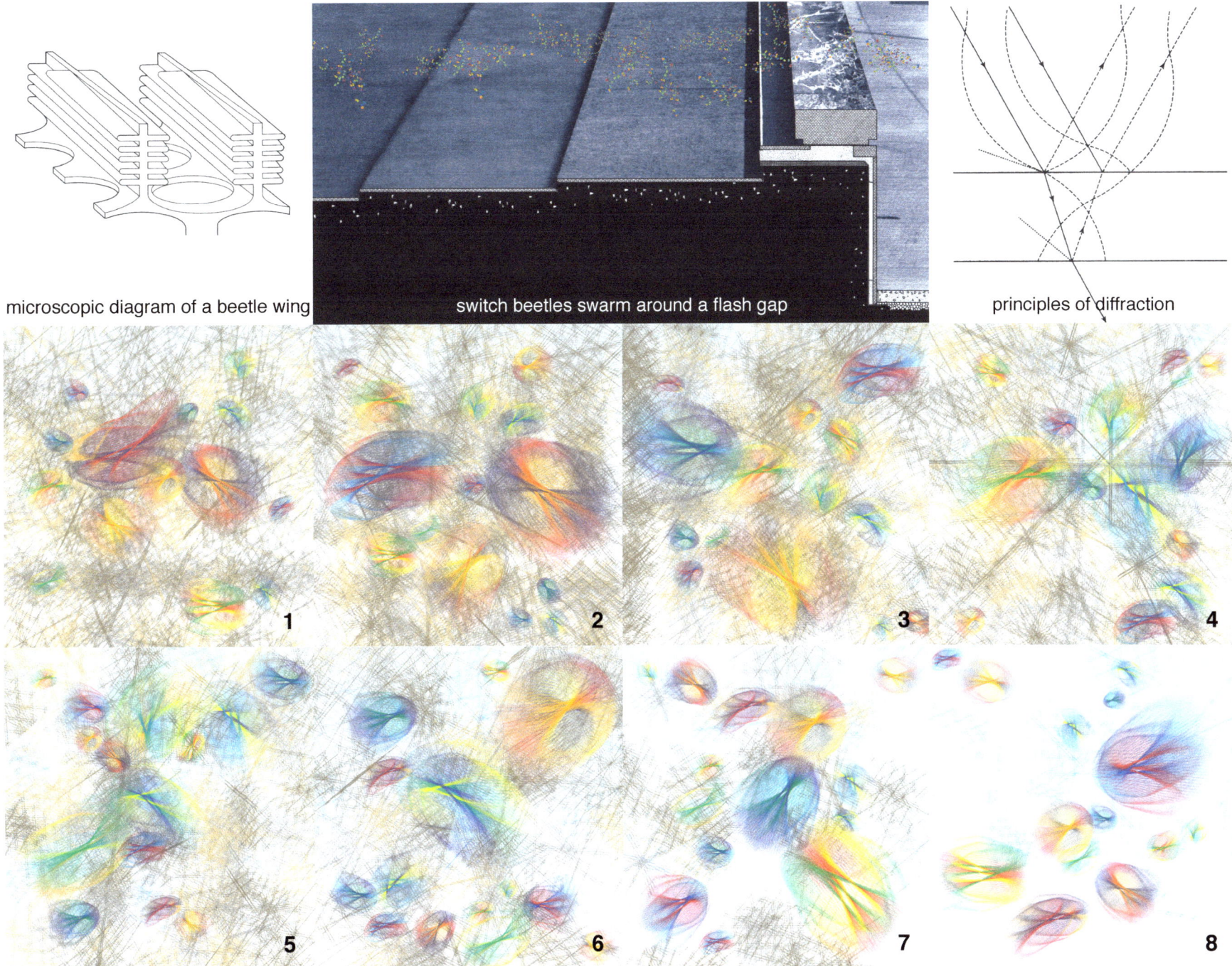

Figure 7/1. The sequence of images 1-8 show a swarm of Switch Beetles gradually eating its way through a volume of polluted air

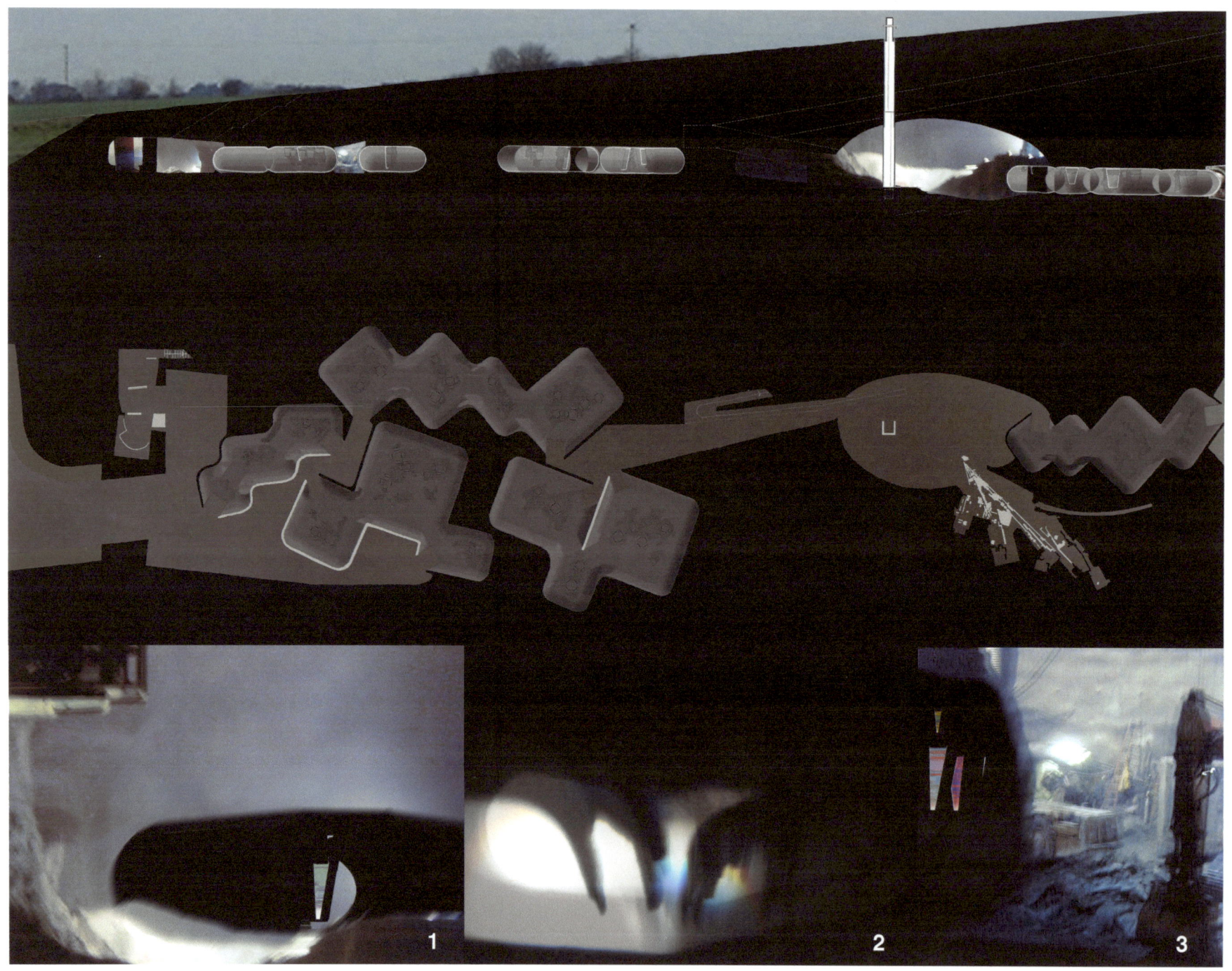

Figure 7/2. DWA's Metaphysical Laboratories in Stevenage, above: section & plan; below: three views of the mixing chamber

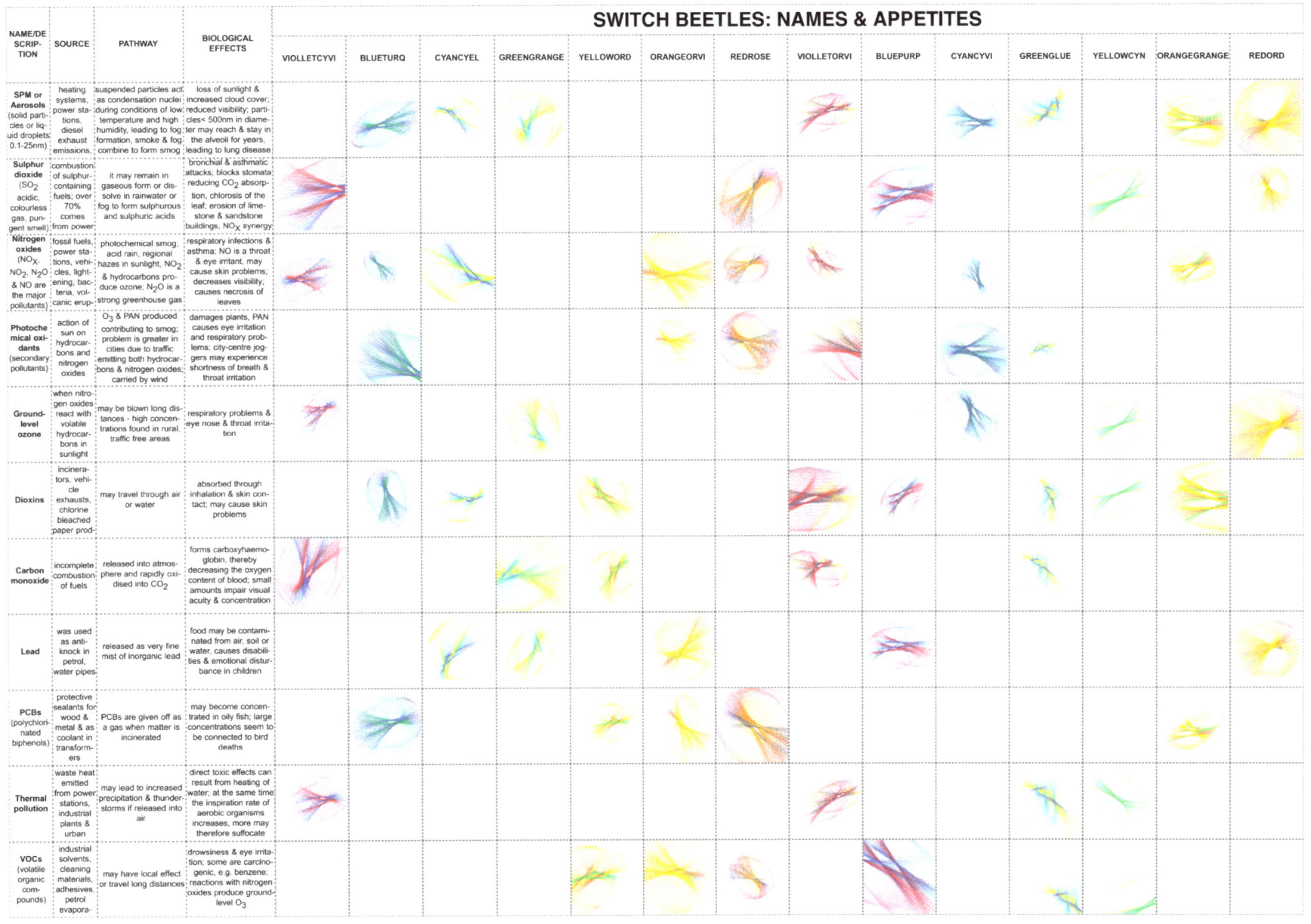

This table was prepared at the DWA laboratory, it lists all of the 14 species of Switch Beetle. The table gives key information about the source, pathway and biological effects of the 11 most common types of pollutants and matches each species of Beetle to the pollutants it consumes, thereby defining their appetite.

Figure 7/3. Table of Beetle Appetites

Figure 7/4. left, generic Beetle dance formation; right: three images of the Beetle dance

Figure 7/5. left: three images of the Beetle dance; right: a Beetle skyscraper taking form at London's Canary Wharf

www.ingramcontent.com/pod-product-compliance
Lightning Source LLC
Chambersburg PA
CBHW042106090526

44590CB00004B/115